I0805899

PRAISE FOR

No Contact

"A landmark work around a theme so prominent—and yet so thoroughly ignored—in modern life. This collection opens chasms beyond writing and testament—but braves toward a new vision of healing, self-dignity, and, most importantly, the possibility for life's flourishing without closure."

—Ocean Vuong, author of *The Emperor of Gladness*

"*No Contact* traces the subtle architecture of absence—echoes that linger in rooms never entered, the strange tenderness that survives even when love is withheld. These essays illuminate the complexity of family with honesty and grit, exploring distance as a kind of seeing and how stepping away can sometimes reveal what staying never could. The authors: warriors. Their words linger, offering a map for anyone who has ever navigated the delicate terrain of love and loss."

—Mira Ptacin, author of *The In-Betweens: The Spiritualists, Mediums, and Legends of Camp Etna*

"In a culture that sanctifies closure, this anthology reminds us that rupture can be beautiful and that closing the door also opens us to new possibilities. *No Contact* bears clear-eyed witness to the cost of leaving, the sacrifice of survival, and the fragile, hard-won freedom that can emerge in the space left behind."

—Kelly McMasters, author of *The Leaving Season: A Memoir*

"This moving collection offers a necessary antidote to the feelings of grief, anger, and shame that often accompany family estrangement. They offer powerful testimonies of how other people navigate the challenges and heartbreaks of difficult families. And they help us see that no matter where we fall on the estrangement continuum, we don't have to go through it alone."

—Harriet Brown, author of *Shadow Daughter: A Memoir of Estrangement*

"In the pages of this beautiful, urgent anthology, I found a community I didn't know I needed. The intimacy in these stories is a salve, as each writer revisits the complex emotions wrought on those of us who dare walk away (and some who are cast out). *No Contact* comes at the right time to heal a generation or two and beyond." —Sonora Jha, author of *Intemperance*

"*No Contact* is safe harbor for anyone who finds themselves unmoored and directionless on the dark sea of estrangement. May these collected essays and poems be a lighthouse for those in need of a guide." —Minda Honey, author of *The Heartbreak Years*

"Call it becoming estranged, going no contact, leaving. Call it saving your life. *No Contact* brings sensitive and searing voices—and nuance—to the conversation about estrangement. An essential anthology for those determined to survive and make it through to the other side."

—Jessica Berger Gross, author of *Estranged: Leaving Family and Finding Home*

No Contact

WRITERS ON ESTRANGEMENT

Edited by Jenny Bartoy

CATAPULT
NEW YORK

NO CONTACT

This is a work of nonfiction. However, some names and identifying details of individuals have been changed to protect their privacy, correspondence has been shortened for clarity, and dialogue has been reconstructed from memory.

Grateful acknowledgment is made for granting permission to reprint the following: "The Uses of Sorrow" by Mary Oliver. Reprinted by permission of The Charlotte Sheedy Literary Agency as agent for the author. Copyright © 2006 by Mary Oliver with permission of Bill Reichblum.

ISBN: 978-1-64622-311-4

Library of Congress Control Number: 2026931343

Cover design by Nicole Caputo
Cover art © Anna Brones
Book design by Laura Berry

Catapult
New York, NY
books.catapult.co

Printed in Canada

10 9 8 7 6 5 4 3 2 1

To those who grieve the living

(In my sleep I dreamed this poem)

Someone I loved once gave me
a box full of darkness.

It took me years to understand
that this, too, was a gift.

—MARY OLIVER, "The Uses of Sorrow"

Contents

Introduction

Estrangement presents an essential existential question: Who are we without our family? What kind of person cuts the proverbial umbilical cord and why? And who do we become once separated from our kin?

Estrangement is the process of making strange what was once known. It is the othering of oneself, the loss of our roots. Estrangement is distance, rupture, silence. It is severance and alienation. One could say that estrangement rewrites our genetic code. It engenders both an orphaning and a metamorphosis.

Estrangement can be grief for our beloveds, still alive but no longer a part of our lives. Estrangement can be liberation and peace too. Release from the ties that bound us. Catharsis. Estrangement can save our lives.

When I cut ties with my father in my twenties, I didn't know what to expect. Along with relief, I felt crushing guilt and shame, and the dissonance overwhelmed me. I knew that the weight that had sat on my chest for years had lifted, that my suicidal ideation had stopped, that the world looked a little brighter. But what daughter cuts off her parent? What kind of monster was I? My father asked me these questions in frequent voicemails and emails. I did not respond—I had told him I wouldn't—but my boundaries didn't yet feel like freedom or peace or even like the right path. Rather, they seemed a precarious barricade, my untethering a temporary solution at best, even if I felt true to myself for the first time ever.

At the time, twenty years ago, I searched for resources to guide me through this breakup with my father, for books representing my experience, or for stories in which I could find solace and connection, but none seemed to exist. The few websites and online articles discussing the topic consistently encouraged adult children to rekindle the relationship with their parent. Hint: I was the problem. But from where I stood, reconciliation did not seem feasible, not until my father changed, and that didn't look likely. I had to find my own way.

My decision was neither wrong nor malevolent. It saved me. Twenty years after cutting ties, I remain "no contact" with my father—and with other family members now, an unwitting consequence. Thanks to therapy, a loving marriage, and supportive friendships, I've learned to stand strong in my boundaries.

Over the years of my estrangement, nothing has validated my heartbreak or my truth more, or propelled my healing further, than connecting with other estranged individuals and hearing their stories. Being open about my experience, I often meet people who are eager to share their own. They too have opted to cut contact; they too were disowned or ghosted by family; they too have grieved their kin through enforced distance. As it turns out, estrangement is quite common. A Cornell University study led by family sociologist Karl Pillemer found that at least 27 percent of American adults are estranged from a family member, and recent elections likely widened the rift.

Estrangement has become an epidemic, according to psychologist Joshua Coleman; and on her podcast, Oprah Winfrey explored the "rising trend" of going no contact. But I question this framing. Estrangement has always existed, because certain families have always treated their members poorly. Just as mental illness and addiction have long torn families apart, there's nothing new about shunning, abandoning, or disowning our own. Black sheep and scapegoats have always walked among us. In other words, family abuse and dysfunction are no modern phenomenon. What seems to have changed in recent years is a growing sense of permission to reject them, a flourishing desire to demand better from our familial relationships.

This shift, I suspect, stems from both the expansion of therapy and the connections fostered by the internet. In therapy, we work toward mental health and clarity. Online, we share our stories, call out bullshit, praise accountability and empowerment, and find supportive communities. A statistical increase in estrangement may simply represent a collective refusal to stay silent or passive in the face of problematic family behavior and chasms in values. That seems objectively healthier than an epidemic. And if estrangement is indeed a widespread ailment, the cure is not simply "less estrangement." We must untangle our roots for meaningful change to happen. Rather than a trend, estrangement is a reckoning.

In recent years, the cultural tide seems to be turning. Memoirs and self-help books now directly address the topic of estrangement, while support groups and social media influencers, even research labs and nonprofit organizations, dedicate their efforts to the matter. Estrangement also pops up in the news with some frequency, though it is too often the subject of articles lacking nuance and judgmental op-eds that dismiss the complexity or validity of the experience.

The glossy lure of a united family remains powerful. It appeals to our most innate sense of belonging. The mending of fractured relationships represents a feel-good conclusion peddled in media and literature alike. Hollywood demands the forgiving, tearful hug between father and daughter and the rueful return of inside jokes between estranged siblings, no matter how toxic their entanglement may prove through a realistic lens. With just a little effort, reunification is within reach, the message goes, no matter how irreparable the rupture or inaccessible the choice may be. This forced "happy ending" presumes that adult family members belong together, that we can solve our differences, that blood is indeed thicker than water. And while reconciliation is undoubtedly desired and, in some cases, achievable for certain families, this trope fails to address a reality faced by countless others.

Estrangement sometimes simply *is*—a stable, not liminal, state of existence in relation to our family systems.

Families fall apart and individuals cut ties for myriad reasons. Estrangement exists on a spectrum. It can be temporary or permanent, mutual or firmly one-sided, focused on one relationship or permeating the entire family tree. But one thing is certain, encompassing nearly all cases: No one wants to be estranged from family. By choice or circumstance, it is simply the only path forward—no matter how painful. The estranged recognize this existential wound in each other and the strength it took to move on. It's a strange sort of club. And we all agree: Estrangement isn't talked about enough.

No Contact immerses readers in an assemblage of narratives that together affirm the complex diversity of the estranged experience. Representation matters—but so does enlightenment. If stories teach us empathy, then a chorus of them can help drive a shift in ingrained perspectives. The voices gathered in this book buck a status quo rooted in the obligation to reconcile in response to estrangement. Shining a light on the many facets of this difficult experience, they focus instead on the resignation, healing, and authenticity found in the rupture from family.

Estrangement is a marginalizing experience, yet it moves in recognizable phases, not unlike the stages of grief. Nearly every estrangement story, writ broadly, follows similar waves and turning points, from rage to acceptance, from devastation to relief. Many among the estranged recall an epiphany and a last straw, an ultimatum letter and a lonely audit, and often a string of uncomfortable conversations with perplexed friends and others. While painfully isolating, the process of estrangement is consistent.

The essays, flash, and poems in this collection run the gamut from harrowing and angry to resolute and reflective, even playful. They demonstrate both the horrors inflicted by kin and the indomitable resilience of the human spirit. Writers share the discoveries they made, the trauma they processed, the voice they found in severing contact with family or having it severed with them. And their collective narrative arc points to hope and possibility.

The stories featured in these pages show that in estrangement, we may lose family, but we can also find ourselves anew—stronger and whole. By sharing these brave voices with you, I hope to spark compassionate thought and deepen the conversation around estrangement. Perhaps in time we may all become better equipped to expect and develop healthy family relationships. In the meantime, peace exists in no contact.

Jenny Bartoy

No Contact

Fractures to Factions

Kate Lewis

The photographs exist before my memories do—our arms slung around our full pack of cousins, gap-toothed grins wide, some summer adventure in the fields behind the house where our grandmothers were once just girls, sisters who ran barefoot through the same grass we stand upon in the images.

Georgia was a place I wore with pride, the beginnings of our whole family flung along one country road, hands dug deep in the well-tilled soil, farming their way to a future.

It felt, back then, like we lived in a different kind of world, one where all the problems of the past had been solved instead of buried, spreading roots beneath the soil, insidious like weeds that choke the crops our families grew.

By college, our photographs are online—you grew thin and reedy, already in the grip of the drugs that would someday end your life, me with my deep Florida tan, hair highlighted from hours of swims in the sun. We swap messages at birthdays, drop comments on photos of each other's weddings, of the births of our children.

As the election approaches, our comments become more

urgent, each of us convinced we can convince the other to share our worldview. We try to change each other's minds online, we become armchair experts of obscure codes in American law. We tell each other we love each other, even as neither of us concedes.

By the first winter of the pandemic, I keep the TV off so my kids won't see, and watch from the small screen in my hand as rioters storm the steps of the Capitol. I'd once walked those steps with my children, their small hands in mine, the future a thing I'd still believed everyone would build together. I watch as people you'd call patriots slam flag poles against the heads of the same police whose role to serve and protect we once vigorously argued over, my hands furious across my laptop in Virginia, yours across your phone screen down South.

The next day, when I search your posts online, it's not for photos of you lifting your kids high for hugs, not to leave a note. This time, when I search your page, I'm scared of what I might find.

Though I'm relieved you were not there, I stop driving down for visits, stop responding to your posts, stop arguing the points that you feel are debatable and I believe are not. For a long time, I stop thinking there might be a way forward, a way to ever heal these fractures that have turned us into factions.

The next photographs posted of you online are those that accompany the news of your death. There we are, arms across each other's shoulders, happy and hopeful. There we are, our bare feet lined with dirt as we dash along that green Georgia grass. There we are, certain that whatever future we faced, we were stronger together.

The Many Meanings of Family Estrangement

Raksha Vasudevan

The therapist was a friend of a friend. A last resort.

"Can you bring to mind a family member who you trust?" she asked. "Maybe a parent or grandparent? A sibling, perhaps?"

I was caught off guard. I couldn't see what this had to do with the unrelenting insomnia that had brought me to her office. But it was an easy question to answer.

"No," I said. "There's no one."

Her blue eyes narrowed. "Really?" she asked. Without giving me a chance to respond, she insisted I must think of someone, for she was going to perform hypnosis to solve the interruptions to my sleep. But for the hypnosis to work, we needed the help of a beloved family spirit.

I should have left then. But I had nowhere to go, no one to seek out. My partner was out of town. Calling family was out of the question. So, I lied. I named my grandparents on my mother's side, though I'd barely known them.

As she proceeded with the hypnosis, pronouncing "pattee"—

Tamil for grandmother—with a long *A* and hard *T*—as "patty," I tried not to cringe. I failed. So, of course, did the hypnosis.

That night, like every night for the previous two weeks, I lay awake. But for once, I wasn't panicking about the long, inky hours ahead, the utter loneliness of being awake while the world around me slept. Instead, I thought about the tale so many still told about family, a tale affirming biological belonging as the ultimate source of care and solace. But though I was not an orphan nor an only child, I had no family I would call as such. Why, I wondered, was this so hard to accept—for others and also, on some level, myself?

I found a new therapist, one who pinpointed family as a source of my anxiety and sleeplessness, rather than its cure. Eventually, with her help, my insomnia resolved. But I'm still trying to figure out how to tell my family story. Not that I want to, necessarily, but America demands it. Explanations are always demanded from women like me, who exist outside the white maleness that is America's baseline for "normal." *Where are you from? Really from! Where is your family? So you're here all by yourself?!*

If immigrants in America are thought to lead lonely lives, misplaced and misunderstood by mainstream society, we are also thought to find refuge in our families. Out there, America can be scary, alienating, confounding. But at home, with the people who share our blood and our language, the people who made the arduous journey from the homeland to here with us or before us, life is bearable again. "I wanted my children to have a better future" and "I wanted to be closer to my parents/children/partner" are the most common immigrant narratives, and also the most accepted: Family reunification is the most direct route to a green card. To come and live in America for family is a legible—and legitimized—desire. But without those ties, the status of "immigrant" is seen as incomprehensible, pitiful, or both. *You must visit your family often! Really, you don't talk to any of them? How sad! But do you think it's more important to be right or to have the relationship? What do you mean you don't want to talk about it?!*

I wonder what kind of explanation would satisfy. Maybe this one: I'm estranged from my dad, because he was physically violent and verbally abusive. That's hard to refute. But what about my mother and brother? How to explain that my efforts with them—visits, cards, calls—are rarely reciprocated? And what's the point in continuing to try if rejection is all but guaranteed—and all the more painful because it's issued by people whose acceptance should be unconditional?

If you were to ask my family members, they might tell a different story—one where I'm the indifferent or insensitive one. Or maybe our stories reach different conclusions. Though I believe my relationship with my mom is best described as estranged, we still text every few weeks, superficial exchanges about the weather, her garden, my dog. And I'm Facebook friends not with my brother but with the profile he and his wife created for their twin boys, now three years old. We've never met.

So, are my mom and I estranged? My brother and I? I'd say yes. They might say no.

All this is to say, my family's stories of family are not the same. I don't know whose version is most true. What I do know is this: I'm tired of trying to find belonging and safety where there's none to be found.

That last statement could have been written by any woman of color fed up with life in America. The alienation that comes with being the first, the token, the "diversity"—that alienation is a second skin for most of us, as familiar as family. And for most of my friends of color, family is how they cope with a culture bent on erasing theirs. They live close or travel often for every birthday, anniversary, and funeral. They cook the foods of their elders. When a natural disaster hits their homeland, they fund-raise. Call it family or culture or legacy, but this is what sustains many of them.

But what about women like me, estranged from both family and the land of our ancestors? We left India when I was ten. I've been back only once, a visit more alienating than any encounter in America. Every relative in Tamil Nadu wanted to know why I didn't speak to my father. They didn't pretend not to know his abusive behavior. Instead, they wanted to know: Didn't he deserve mercy?

"Didn't I?" I wanted to ask. But I stayed silent, because I understood. For my relatives, who lived in multigenerational homes, whose social lives were defined by visits with extended family and whose plethora of upper-caste privileges were handed down through family lines, estrangement must seem a horrible fate—topped only by being estranged in a foreign land. Surrounded by strangers, in every sense. To them, that must seem a fate worse than death. Sometimes, it seems that way to me too.

People think estrangement is a final state, unchangeable and totalizing. For that reason, some also see it as the easy way out: Being in a relationship with someone—anyone—is inherently messy. Severing the tie cleans things up once and for all.

I wish it were that simple, that static. It's not. Estrangement, for me, has been an ever-shifting constellation of regrets and loyalties and, yes, joys. It wouldn't be so painful if I didn't remember the feeling of curling up with my mother after a nightmare, or my father and I singing along to the Eagles, our voices gloriously off-key. If I didn't remember my brother putting his skinny twelve-year-old body between me and our father during one of his rages.

Estrangement wouldn't be so painful if I didn't remember the intimacy that was once there.

Growing up, I used to fantasize about new family: a tight circle of friends or a partner whose family would welcome me into their fold. Now, at thirty-four, I'm lucky to have both those things. But neither have lessened the pain of estrangement. Sometimes they've even deepened it. Like when my partner's parents talk about their daughter's boyfriend's family—how welcoming they are, how tight-knit they are. Their faces light up: One of their children is with someone from a good family.

Or this past summer, attending a friend's wedding. My partner and I were recently engaged, and I was taking notes on everything: yes to an outdoor ceremony, no to having two officiants. But as I watched my friend's father walk her down the aisle, there was nothing to catalog but the grief quietly enveloping me. At first, I chalked it up to the question of who would give me away—certainly not my father. Would my brother or mom even come? I wasn't sure. The real question, I realized, was not who would give me away but who—and what—I belonged to, a question that surfaced again later that night, when generations of her family converged on the dance floor, swaying furiously to Tajik tunes in a frenzied celebration of their childhood and country and culture. I wanted to join them like the other guests, I really did, and I would have if I weren't having trouble breathing, my lungs feeling full of some invisible fluid.

Since then, I haven't done any wedding planning. The thought of exposing these gaping holes—in my family, or lack thereof; in my culture, or lack thereof—has kept me terrified and dithering, incapable of entering a new tale of family. And even when I do, I know the old story will still be there, bleeding through the page.

These days, I'm less interested in creating a narrative of belonging that's legible to America than in claiming what already belongs to me. My mother tongue, for one. I've started relearning Tamil, a process that's surprising me, surfacing a different part of myself—playful, innocent, curious. Maybe the part that first came into consciousness.

That's the other thing that helps: The photo I keep by my desk. It was taken in Chennai when I was five or six years old, blue-frocked and chubby-cheeked. My brother is sitting next to me, his smile showing his lost baby teeth. In the background, my mother is a sari rushing by. My father must have taken the photo. I can feel his presence hovering outside the frame.

Every time I look at this photo, I feel a surge of tenderness—for my brother, for my parents, for Chennai. For the intimacy we once had. And more than any grief or resentment, that reminds me of why I won't—can't—return to them. Distance is the only way I know to preserve that tenderness. The only way, too, to protect the self I see in that photo, her bright eyes, her open, unafraid face. Estrangement is the only way to keep from becoming a stranger to myself.

You Don't Have to Be Good

Domenica Ruta

Not long after I was diagnosed with cancer, my father and I had the biggest fight of our lives. "I am done," I yelled into the phone, "you are dead to me." And before I could hang up, he got in the last word.

"Good."

I didn't mean what I had said to my father. Quite the opposite. I was free-falling in an existential abyss, flailing for something, anything, to hold on to, and rage was an easy tether back to life. Love would have been better, but I'd take what I could get.

I believe, given our history, that my father meant his last word to me. It's possible these are the last words we will ever speak to each other.

In the summer of 2021, I'd felt a lump in my left breast. I had just weaned my second child from nursing, and the doctor assured me that was the cause but ordered a mammogram just in case. The mammogram warranted a biopsy, and then a week later,

I got a text message via the MyChart app that read "Invasive Ductal Carcinoma."

This is not good. It was the most complex thought I could produce. A sensation like falling, falling without end, had wrenched my thinking self away. There was no doctor available that day to give me a prognosis, and it would be weeks before I could see an oncologist who could deliver the news: stage 1 (good), high grade (bad).

While waiting for this appointment, my husband and I paced around our apartment, a pair of red-eyed ghosts, gritting our teeth as we lied to our children. When the fear in me had reached a desperate pitch, I called my father.

I knew this was probably a bad idea. Every once in a while, my father could shock me with his generosity. He has the mettle of a New England construction worker who knows how to tough out physical pain. But he is also someone who could snap without warning. He beat the shit out of my mother, my stepmother, my brother, but never me, my sister, or our family dog, setting up a bizarre template of loyalties and expectations for those who loved him. It was our family cycle to have violent ruptures—Dad throwing punches, hurling blame, promising worse to come—followed by silences of a few days or weeks, then a return to an anxious normality in which we all acted like nothing happened.

He was seldom moved by the vulnerabilities of others, least of all his children's. As a kid, I could vomit until I retched yellow wads of bile, and he would accuse me of faking it. I once fractured my ankle, with an X-ray to prove it, and he said my crutches were a cry for attention. But the word *cancer* had unhooked all these memories from my mind. I'd been working so hard to be a sturdy mother for my kids; I wanted, just for a moment, to be parented.

"Don't be dramatic," my father said when I broke down crying and confessed I was afraid I was going to die. Though he must have considered it serious, as he mentioned the possibility of driving down from Boston to visit soon. "I'm gonna have to come down," he repeated on the phone, as if trying to convince himself.

"Please," I blubbered. "That would be so great. The kids need to run around in the park, and we can't see straight right now."

He couldn't come that weekend as he was tired, he said. And not the following weekend either; he had dinner plans with his new wife's parents, people who lived fifteen minutes from his house, people he saw nearly every weekend. People, I might add, who didn't have cancer.

"Later," he told me. "I'll come down later."

Later, I would have to ask my sister, who was getting married that year: "Are all of your wedding guests vaccinated?" Six out of the one hundred were not. "Could you tell them your sister has cancer? That I'm on chemo and my oncologist said it wasn't safe to be indoors with unvaccinated people?" Surely that could change their minds. I wasn't asking her to uninvite them, though that is what I would have done for her, immediately, without needing to be asked. She saw things differently.

Again, I reached out to our father. "Please, talk to her. Make her understand."

"Everyone has a right to make their own choices," he replied, "and you are choosing not to come to your sister's wedding." But I wasn't choosing; I was being forced out, I explained. "Don't be dramatic," he said, reprising his favorite song. And we started fighting.

I got what I had been seeking—to feel like a child being parented. A teenager, more accurately, who was pushing her dad away in a sick hope that he would do the opposite and hold her tight. *You're dead to me*, that teenager screamed, and the parent said, *Good*.

I had already been estranged from my mother for over a decade at this point, and she in turn was estranged from her family of origin. It feels like a folktale to remember it now—that the two of us were once a part of something much larger. My mother's family had managed to hold on to the last shreds of that old immigrant cloth, the big Sunday dinner, with children running wild, tables too crowded with food to set plates down, my grandmother and my aunts singing bawdy Sicilian folk songs.

My mother was always getting herself cut off from one sibling or another. She was volatile and narcissistic and said every single horrible thought in her head out loud. Every once in a while, however, her vicious indictments of her siblings were actually true. Either way, she'd get put in the penalty box, with me alongside her, and we'd hover outside the family for an indefinite period of time until we were allowed back in. Then, at some point in my adolescence, the estrangement became permanent. All my aunts and uncles and cousins disappeared from her life and mine as well. Estrangement didn't start with me. You could say it's an inheritance.

This is part of the reason why, despite the urging of every therapist I'd ever had, it took so long to go no contact with my mother. I couldn't leave her all alone. She had no one else. Like a battered wife, I broke up with her in stages, setting a boundary, feeling guilty, coming back. She'd threaten suicide, and I would go to her house and let her scream at me until her will to live was renewed; then, as soon as she'd nodded off, I'd escape.

After one such episode I drove bleary-eyed to my father's house. Shopping for oranges at the hardware store, this impulse is called in certain circles. He couldn't stand what he saw in me that day—tears, a runny nose, his failure to protect me, perhaps. He roared with his face a hot breath away from mine, punched the wall behind my head. His fist flew past my ear. I flinched. "Where are the cameras, drama queen?" he sneered, then imitated my expression, my scared little yelp.

Years after I stopped speaking to my mother, I published a book about her, hoping with a childish logic that she would read it and it would change her. She'd get sober, she'd get help, things would be different. Another folktale. In that same book, I gave my father a kind of hero's arc, in part because it was narratively satisfying; I worried the story would be too bleak if I plumbed the true depths of both my parents' brutality. But mostly I was writing an insurance policy. I'd already lost my mother, and by extension, I'd lost my stepfather, the kindest of my four parents, a man I loved very much, as well as what remained of our extended family, the collateral damage of estrangement. That losing her was a choice, my choice, did little to soften the guilt and grief I felt on a daily basis.

I couldn't lose my father too. How much would that hurt? Could I survive it?

In the span of a month, I was diagnosed with cancer; then our apartment building was sold, and the new owners wanted us to move as soon as possible, so we moved. A week later, with things still in cardboard boxes, I had a double mastectomy and my older son changed schools.

On weekends, my children watched videos from sunup to sundown. We ate greasy food with our hands and no napkins so that all our clothes got oil stains and we looked dirty and disheveled even when we were clean. The baby got a bath—maybe weekly? His hair grew into his face, covering his eyes. Most nights we were too tired to fight him and handed him a bag of Goldfish for dinner. One morning the six-year-old brought a whole pan of brownies into my bed and ate them, laughing, because he knew we would do nothing to stop him. One afternoon my husband burst into deep, shuddering tears while eating a peanut butter and jelly sandwich. "I'm so scared you're going to die," he said.

The baby needed near-constant attention, but most of all, he needed to be picked up and held, the one thing I couldn't do with my gouged-out chest. And so he learned with a quickness that broke my heart to grab a pillow first, then barrel toward me with some cushioning for our hugs. The first grader woke up every night and thundered down the hall into my room, where he climbed, panting, into bed with us. His skinny arms and legs wrapped around me tight, as if I would fly away if he loosened his grip even a little.

In daylight, I asked him if he had questions or scary thoughts he wanted to talk about. He said no. He drew dozens, quite possibly hundreds, of pictures of Thomas the Tank Engine mutilated by nuclear fallout. Thomas exploding in flames. Thomas crying tears of blood.

I let him draw on my bald head with magic marker. I let him stay up watching movies too old for him because it was too late, he was already old now. He learned to read and write that year. "My momme got btr frm her sgre," he scrawled between the dotted lines of his workbook. The baby grew more beautiful by the day, entering the big bang of language, naming all the objects and actions in our home. "Mumma go to the doctor," he said every time my hand touched the door.

Dying was not my worst fear. That my children would lose their mother was.

A point of pride before getting cancer was that I never got sick. I used to brag about my immune system as though it were microscopic proof of my goodness. Except when it wasn't. For years, my body had a tradition of shutting down every Christmas, when I'd get walloped by a nasty flu. One such Christmas, I felt a virus crisscrossing my throat as I boarded a plane to Boston, and by the time it landed, I was feverish and aching.

I was practicing my escape from my mother that year. This meant sleeping at my father's house, a place I was legally supposed to have lived 50 percent of my childhood but never did, a place where I hadn't had my own bed since I was fourteen. At that time, I was in good standing with my father, as good as anyone could be. He always loved when I hated my mother. So I assumed it was safe to ask for a ride home from the airport.

As soon as I climbed into his truck that night, I could tell he was mad at me. He wouldn't look at me. Grumbled when I said hello. Sped away from the curb as soon as I'd shut the door and before I'd fastened my seat belt.

"I think I have the flu," I said.

"No you don't," he answered in a voice so confident I wondered for a second if I had hallucinated my symptoms. He turned up the radio, a finicky AM station broadcasting the hockey game he was missing on TV because of me. We drove for thirty minutes to his house in silence. Once home, he hopped out and I asked him to help me carry my bags inside. He paused in the driveway, a snarl curling his lips. "No," he said and slammed the door. I slept that night on the living room couch, which was covered in dirt and salt tracked in by the family dog. I had to shove her sleeping body off the only blanket, an itchy acrylic afghan that smelled like shit.

Why did I think any of this would change simply because I had cancer?

It had been a few months since my initial diagnosis, a few months since I'd stopped speaking to my father. He had walked my sister down the aisle at her unvaccinated wedding. Everyone was living happily ever after without me. My doctor ordered some follow-up scans that revealed a suspicious mass on my hip bone.

"Could it be that the cancer has spread to my bones?" I asked my doctor.

"We'll need to do more scans," she answered.

I wanted to pick up a loaded gun and shoot myself in the forehead. This is terror-logic: to be so afraid of dying that you want to die. My brain was brittle with terror, and I was striking a match, ready to torch it. "I want to kill myself," I whispered under my breath. The words slipped out like drool. Shameful. Insane.

This was not the first time I'd found myself on the edge of existence, dangling a foot over the cliff. In my late twenties, a few years after cutting off my mother, I drank myself into a darkness so deep I couldn't get out. At night, I prayed to a god I didn't believe in to explode my liver in my sleep so that I could die without having to put in the work. In a semi-lucid moment I realized my polluted liver might last years despite my best efforts, leaving the end up to me. So I made a plan to jump in front of a commuter train a few blocks from my apartment where the tracks were frighteningly accessible. Not drinking felt like the bigger sacrifice.

But there were these people who gathered together in the basements of churches and synagogues, and listening to them tell stories made me feel a little better for the hour that I sat with them. I showed up on their turf a complete stranger, and they welcomed me in with terrible coffee in a paper cup. I would shake and cry and scratch the poison out of my skin, and old ladies would move their seat to be near me, holding me still with their strong arms and feeding me brownies until my hands were steady enough to feed myself. Men who looked and sounded like my father would ask me how I was doing and then shock me by listening to the answer.

It didn't make any sense. I was a mess and not a hot one, a drunk who repeated the same unfunny, sometimes offensive joke even louder when no one laughed the first time. I was constantly burping a little bit of puke into my mouth. I felt entitled to a stiff drink first thing in the morning, as I had a big day ahead of doing nothing, contributing nothing. These people knew all that, and they seemed to love me. It was repulsive at first, the way they said they loved me, showed it in acts of service freely given without keeping score, and in that repulsion, I felt myself falling again in dark space, which is another way to say I was powerless. The gravity of their love pulled me until I had to accept I was never getting rid of these people, no matter what heinous things I confessed out loud, no matter how much doubt and hate, mostly for myself, spewed from my mouth. Then I did the unthinkable—admitted I needed their help, admitted that I *had needs*—and this made them love me even more. And through the love of these people, everything changed. I didn't become good, but I started to get better.

I got more scans to investigate the mass on my hip, and then I waited. At night I would Google my mortality then walk around my dark apartment to see if everyone was still breathing. Standing in the doorway of my son's room, I watched him sleep on the bottom bunk of his bed, blankets kicked off, at least one limb pushed deliberately into the cozy slim gap between the bed frame and the wall. The baby slept with my husband in our bed. I didn't sleep anywhere because I couldn't sleep.

My son's eyes are stunning, large and round, fringed in dark, long lashes, the kind that will make lovers act foolish one day. In daylight, his eyes get all the attention, so it is only in sleep, with eyes sealed shut, that the beauty of his nose, his full pink lips stands out. I would stand there entranced by his face, unable to move.

How could a parent see their child in vulnerability—such as sleep, such as cancer—and feel anything but wild, desperate love?

After months of not speaking, my father broke the silence. A phone call I sent to voicemail then listened to immediately. It was doubtful he was sorry, but maybe he missed me. I would have taken that. I would have taken almost anything.

The brother of his new wife had died, he said in his message. "I thought you should know."

An odd entry point, for sure. I had never met this brother-in-law, and my father had never mentioned him; in fact, I knew his wife had a sister but had not heard anything about a brother. This display of solemnity was out of character for my father, enough to give me pause.

Proximity to death works a way into even the most obdurate human heart, and maybe this new brother-in-law had led my father out to the brink of existence, where I had been hanging around lately. Maybe he got a glimpse of me there, fighting for my life, and it inspired him to reach out.

Then it hit me. There had been a death in the family. People would be gathering, most likely at his home. They would ask my father about his children, his daughter, recently married.

"And the other one?" they would ask. The one with cancer.

"I just called her today," he could say without lying. "She's good."

Love in my family is one thing in three parts, like the Catholic Trinity, deliberately baffling to scare away the weak: You have to earn it; you earn it by being good; your goodness is measured by how little you need.

It wasn't the good grades that impressed my parents but the way I did my homework without being told. The made bed, the dishes drying in the rack, no one ever had to ask. I could entertain myself alone for hours, days, whole summers without complaining. The only compliment my father has ever paid me is how self-sufficient I was at a very young age. That's one way to put it. I ground my teeth, clenched my fists, aged in fast motion, trying to be invisible enough for my father to see me.

So with cancer, I tried even harder. I beat myself in the face with gratitude. I was so lucky to have health care and a healthy husband and healthy children! To be white and educated and taken seriously by my doctors. I made microdonations to every single cause that popped up on social media. I memorized every person's name at the cancer center, the front desk staff, the phlebotomists, the scores of nurses. I asked them about their days, how *they* were doing. If they seemed game, I made hilarious jokes. I made them laugh! When people asked me how I was doing then, I would kill them with my smile.

At chemo, the nurses asked me if I felt any pain. Neuropathy like stinging nettles shot from my feet up to my shins. My hands curled inward from cramping.

"I'm good!" I would say each time. "Just a little tired. But it's not bad."

Over the course of my treatment, most of the church basements were still closed due to COVID, so we met daily on Zoom instead. When people asked me what I needed, I said nothing. Recovering liars themselves, they saw right through me.

"You're only as sick as your secrets" was their patient reminder. And so I admitted I was too ashamed to ask for help because I didn't think I deserved it.

Cancer had been a test of my strength and morals, and I had failed. According to my family of origin, I was supposed to rise to the occasion, Christlike, imbued with otherworldly understanding and forgiveness. But here I was, wanting, if not attention—that was too much, a mortal sin—then an acknowledgment of what I was going through, that it was hard and scary, that even if I had proven myself to be good, to be strong, to be self-sufficient, that I still needed a little something more under the circumstance. What kind of person wants all that? A selfish, needy person. Someone whose wickedness caused her to get cancer. Someone who didn't deserve to live.

So I asked for nothing. And these people from the church basements gave me an embarrassment of riches: a big beautiful monstera; homemade food delivered to my door in Tupperware that didn't need to be returned, lots of cheesy, carby things my family could pick at for days in fugue states of terror and grief; a house cleaner who came twice a month; high-end mastectomy bras; gift cards for cosmetics and massages and food; various teas, all of them infused with the hope that such problems could be borne with a hot drink; handmade cards and lots of hats for my bald head; several pairs of the comfiest socks; chocolates—lots and lots of chocolates; pendants and prayer cards blessed by nuns in Calcutta; childcare, the most essential gift of all; laundry washed, dried, and folded; texts and phone calls all day, every day; thousands of therapeutic memes; things I would feel guilty for not remembering now except for the fact that the givers made clear these gifts were not transactional, they were given with the understanding that we were overwhelmed, given with purest love.

The newest scans came back clean—the mass on my hip just a bone spur, not metastasis. I wanted to tell my father, still hoping for that rare glimpse of his generosity, but it was not worth the more likely accusation of drama. So I texted about fifty other people instead, my chosen family from the basements and the Zoom meetings, and in turn, they texted fifty more.

"Thank you," I said to them, the ones who prayed to their higher powers for me.

Despite this good outcome, I don't know if I believe in god. I don't know if I even believe in the energetic field supposedly whooshed around by prayer. But I believe in these people, who rushed into my heart like it was a building on fire to save me, again and again, and in an inextinguishable self that wants to love and be loved despite all evidence against taking such risks.

I want to say that the COVID-19 vaccine is what finally tore my family apart. This would locate us in History with a capital *H*, among a network of American families gutted by the ideological wars of our dying republic. This belief would provide me with a political bypass for my pain. If it's political, then it is not my fault, and I am not alone—the two biggest fears of my childhood.

The truth is our fight was about responsibility and loyalty, about my sister's wedding and my cancer, our vulnerabilities and needs, but like any family fight, like all of them, it is a fight with the past. My impulse to flatten people into hateful, uncaring monsters because it's too painful to integrate that they can love me and still hurt me like this. It's about my sister's revulsion toward my needs, which she learned from our father, who learned it from someone else, I may never know who. Ghosts of ourselves, wounded and resentful, screaming into the wind, hoping at last to be heard.

My needs in that time were too much for my family of origin, but maybe they were too much for any family. With or without estrangement, the nuclear family is pretty small. Three to five people on average. So maybe it's not a problem of politics or past trauma but one of numbers, and a nuclear family is simply too small to contain all that this poisoned earth dumps inside it. The community I found in the church basements is big enough, vast, like a sky full of stars, always there, in daylight and in the dark.

The Stripping of Threads

Jamal Mahjoub

When my brother first came out, I would make an effort to go and visit him. Back then he was living in a grotty house in Earl's Court—an area he had no connection to but where he would remain for the next twenty years. All of his stuff had been lost when he failed to pay his former landlord. The guitars, records, books, clothes: All of it was either thrown away or sold when he went to prison. He was given a tiny room at the bottom of a house inhabited by other ex-convicts. In the hallways you stepped aside for former offenders with no idea of what they might have done to wind up here. Some of them were violent, one threatened my brother with a knife.

The room was a self-contained flat with a filthy bathroom that you had to squeeze into sideways. It had an old sash window that offered a view of a brick-lined light well. High walls you had no chance of seeing over. Compared to prison it might have been a step up, but it was a short one. These places are meant to give people a foothold in society, a chance to improve their situation. He never tried. As if the will to move on had somehow deserted him, he settled there, signed on for unemployment benefits, and collected his daily methadone. That was it. In the beginning I suggested he move out of London, which is expensive, especially if you have no money. I suggested the South Coast. Fresh air, less congestion, probably a better chance of finding work. He wasn't interested.

He was completely isolated. He had no friends that I knew of, no family nearby, nothing around him. Old friends he had known back in Khartoum would ask after him. One or two even tried to look him up. It never came to anything, and eventually they stopped asking. Distant relatives would inquire, but they too stopped. It was basically understood that every family has one who goes astray. Bring him back here, they said. We'll take care of him. But going back to Sudan was the last thing he would do. Go back home with nothing to show for it. So he remained there, lost in the transit hall that is London's maze. The most regular employment he found was volunteering twice a week at a charity bookshop, but that was the zenith of his ambitions. His education was wasted. There seemed no chance of him recovering his vocation of being an architect. And the dreams he'd once had, of becoming a famous musician, were now never mentioned.

Our parents were gone by then. When my father passed away, we contacted the prison to see if we could break the news in person. We all sat in the visiting room on plastic chairs that were bolted to the floor. It was clear that he wasn't happy to see us. The resentment was palpable, clinging to him like stale sweat. He had guessed why we had come, he said. It was as if he couldn't wait for the visit to be over and for us to leave. We were a reminder of a previous existence, one that he had turned away from and that was painful for him to see again.

By the time he came out, my mother had also passed. Whenever I was in London, I would mark off a day to go over to Earl's

Court and visit him. We would go for a drink, or maybe a meal. He was my little brother, after all. When my children were small, I sometimes took them along with me, though they didn't really understand who he was. He rarely showed much interest and had trouble remembering their names. I felt I owed this much at least, if not to him, then to the parents who had created and raised us. I was bearing the torch for my father, who used to visit him every Friday after mosque. At the time I had been angry about this. It seemed to me that my father was trying to pretend that everything was the same as it had always been, rather than face the facts. My brother, after all, had arguably contributed to their ill health. One of the hardest things I ever did in my life was to tell my father that his son was not only taking hard drugs but probably selling them and that he and my mother needed to be careful. My brother was living with them at the time. I had witnessed the shame my father had felt to see his own son tried and convicted in a British court, a country in which he had spent much of his life trying to prove how civilized and respectable a Black man could be.

In the end duty wasn't enough. My brother saw through my efforts. He accused me of trying to fulfill an obligation, and of course he was right to an extent. I also realized that I, like my father, wanted to pass a couple of hours with him in something resembling normality. The meetings became more strained, and gradually they tapered off. There came a point when it was no longer worth making the effort, when our conversations would invariably veer into argument and bitter acrimony. And so it ended. Since then, we have not had any direct contact. I don't see him. He doesn't write or call. He never replied to my emails, so I stopped sending them. I have no telephone number for him. From time to time I hear from my middle brother that he is still alive, but that's about it. And the same goes the other way. I am, I think, literally dead to him.

How did it all come to this? I can't help thinking that when we were small the three of us were very close. There are only eighteen months between each of us. After five years without children, my mother suddenly had three boys in quick succession. We were brought up in the same household, played together, shared a room when we were small, went to the same school, slept outside under the same stars. It would be wrong to say we were treated equally. All parents may aspire to impartiality, but in the end factors like character and affinity play a role. They tried, I suppose, but I always thought my father was harder on me as the eldest and favored my younger brother because he was small and cute. He had a nickname for him, whereas he often mocked me. Perhaps that's just the way I remember it. I left home early and my brother stayed late. Our middle brother found his own course, marrying into a rather conservative and wealthy Egyptian family that adopted him wholeheartedly. Not so much gaining a daughter as losing a son, my mother would say. Under their influence he turned to Islam, something we had not been encouraged to do as children. Neither of my parents were firm believers. My mother was at best a skeptic. She hated the hypocrisy of pious people right up to the very end, while my father became gradually more observant, doubling up the five daily prayers to make up for lost time and making the hajj to Mecca.

How can three souls, born to the same parents within such a narrow time frame and brought up in identical surroundings, find themselves so alienated from one another that they can no longer bear to see each other, and rarely even communicate? This is the question that I keep coming back to, the one I can never quite explain. Only three people in the world shared that specific experience of growing up together, and yet we cannot get along. Whatever bond or allegiance was formed in those early years, it was not powerful enough to overcome our personal choices.

I wonder what measure of this is mine to bear. I wasn't there, after all, in those crucial years when my brother went from a teenager to an adult. I had been awarded a scholarship, which I saw as my ticket to see the world. I was determined to travel as widely as possible, and shut the idea of home out of my mind. I assumed it would always be there for me to return to. But those intervening years were key for him. He discovered a new kind of notoriety, hanging out with people who were older than him, expats for whom Sudan was just a dangerous playground. He fell in with an English guy who set up an illicit bar. Alcohol was banned at the time, but they brought booze in overland from the Eritrean port of Massawa. There were checkpoints on the roads, but it was easy enough to circumvent them by cutting across the desert. Through that gateway came other things, including heroin. When things got too hot for him, he came to London to join me. By then he already had a problem.

In the end, my mother had no need for my warning. She worked it out for herself. She had just been diagnosed with melanoma and was in London for treatment. She threw herself into trying to understand my brother's problem. She attended meetings for parents of addicts and read countless books on the subject, believing there had to be a way to cure him. It's a natural instinct to try and protect your children from harm, but it was already too late. People get clean because they want to. You can't make them do it. I see now that I had been doing the same thing. Those visits to Earl's Court were my attempt to understand. And like my father, I was trying to normalize the situation. Perhaps subconsciously I even believed that I would find the cure, that I could fix the problem. I was also looking for a way to forgive him, for what he'd done to the family, to our parents, for squandering the opportunities he'd been given. When eventually I stopped going, it had become clear to me that I was deceiving myself. I could never forgive him. This thing would always be there between us. I would never understand, and I could never save him from himself.

Eventually he resolved his addiction problems, or at least brought them under control, but he remains caught within the narrow confines of his choices, still unable to move on. He burrowed down into the idea that this was meant to be, this was what marked him out as being special. His acceptance of his fate and those broken dreams he'd made so little effort to achieve contains no small degree of martyrdom, which is tied to a notion of redemption. The reason it is so hard to forgive him is that although he cannot deny the pain he has caused, he cannot really bring himself to admit it. Underlying everything there rankled a feeling of injustice, a sense that life had let him down, dealt him a bad hand. In his narrative he is always the victim. Our parents are to blame for not instilling in him more discipline. If he lacked inner strength, it was because they had been too easy on him. This obsession with self that borders on narcissism goes some way to explaining the resentment, toward me, toward our parents, toward the world for putting obstacles in his way. It's what makes it impossible for him to have more than a passing interest in anyone else's life. In the end, the only subject left to him is himself.

For a number of years he persisted in the belief that he could somehow vindicate himself, turn his plight into noble sacrifice. With his share of the inheritance, which wasn't a lot, he invested in the stock market, something he knew nothing about. In due course all the money was lost, but for a long time he would tell me, rather dramatically, that if something should happen to him, the financial documents were in an ugly old briefcase he kept in a corner of his room. That was his plan, to finally make good on everything by paying back what was, in his mind at least, some kind of fortune. Ignoring the fact that no amount of money would ever make up for the heartache and pain he had caused.

I hold no illusions about us being reunited. All of this has gone on for far too long. The threads that connected us have been shorn off. All that remains is the memory of it and the unresolved mystery about what it all means. Maybe we were simply too close. We know too much about each other. There is a time when we were at school in Khartoum that always comes back to me. We used to have extra Arabic lessons in the afternoons. My father would drive us over to the teacher's house and we would sit in the yard, which was just a small, bare space between the rooms and the whitewashed outer wall. We sat around a table covered with a plastic sheet. One afternoon my brother made a lot of mistakes. I think we were doing dictation. The teacher told him off for not working hard enough. Without a word, my brother got up and ran to the tall metal street door and pulled it open. We watched in amazement, then we all got up and went over to take a look. The house was surrounded by sandy streets and opposite was a football pitch. Again, just a dusty space with a goal frame at either end. The lines were marked in chalk. There he was, halfway across, running through the bemused players with no regard for the shouts that followed him. Where's he going, the teacher asked, speaking our thoughts aloud. The teacher's younger brother took off and eventually brought him back. It was a funny story at the time, but it always made me wonder. We were far away from where we lived, and he didn't have a clue how to get back home. So where was it he thought he was going? I don't think he knew. All he wanted was to get away from where he was and maybe never come back. It was as simple as that.

The Cost of a Mother

Hannah Bae

"Your mother called," the office secretary says in Korean. She intercepts me as I head to my desk in the *JoongAng Daily* newsroom at the start of my shift. "She seemed worried, and she was asking where you were."

I feel a prickle of embarrassment. I'm twenty-two, a junior copyeditor, and the youngest person on staff at my Seoul newspaper. I yearn to be taken seriously. I take care to dress neatly in conservative shift dresses. I trace my eyes in tasteful makeup with exacting precision. I wear my competence for all to see.

"Joesong hapnida," I apologize by reflex as I lower my eyes to my ballet flats. I know that if Umma is calling, it can't be good. I imagine her blubbering over the phone in manic, incoherent Korean to the mystified secretary, and I cringe.

I am only a few months into my prestigious Princeton journalism fellowship in South Korea, so I continue in broken, toddler-level Korean, attempting to smooth things over: "I'm so sorry. She has my cell phone number. I don't know why she would call here to talk to me . . ."

"She was very worried," the secretary repeats before she shuffles back to her desk.

I am learning that strict Confucianism governs Korean society. Here, family means everything—one bad actor can heap disgrace on an entire bloodline.

By this point in life, I am afraid of my mother. For years, her mind has felt broken. I know something is wrong with Umma, but my family says that whenever they bring up treatment, she refuses. "Crazy? Who you call crazy?" I picture her shouting at them defensively. Mental illness carries deep stigma among Koreans, and I doubt my family can afford treatment anyway.

I've moved to Seoul, as far away from Umma as I can get. The physical distance between Korea and our home in Virginia keeps me from getting sucked into her damaging spiral that drags the rest of my family down.

Her phone call to the newsroom feels like a performance for anyone who will give her attention. She acts out her concern for her young daughter living alone a continent away, and I look like the callous one, presumably so out of touch and unavailable that my own mother has to track me down at work. But I know the truth: She hasn't shown up for me for years. She did not attend my high school graduation or move me into my college dorm. She left me abandoned in parking lots, an afterthought of a child waiting for rides that would never come. She let our father beat my sisters and me. She opened the apartment door and stepped aside when Child Protective Services took us into foster care.

I stew during my copyediting shift that night. I don't want to call her back, but Korean duty continually pulls, deep inside my chest. When I get back to my apartment at 10:30 p.m., I dial my parents' number. It's 9:30 a.m. on the East Coast, but no one picks up.

I'm a sophomore pacing around a fountain on my college campus in Miami, hiccupping with sobs as I call home. I've just left the registrar's office, where I've been turned away from signing up for next semester's classes because I owe back tuition.

As I wait for my parents to pick up, the sunlight beams down onto perfectly manicured beds of palms and hibiscus that match my soft pink sundress, but I feel black and hurt inside.

"Hel-loh." The accented staccato of Appa's voice finally comes through.

I tell him about the bounced check. "You told me to focus on school," I say accusingly. "You told me I didn't have to worry about money." Between me and my sisters, I'm the only one to go to college.

"Mi-an, mi-an," he apologizes. He'll put a new check in the mail soon. He says it'll never happen again. But it does.

In 2008, frightening headlines about the plummeting global markets streak across the *JoongAng Daily*, the *International Herald Tribune*, and screens tuned to CNN International. Umma's calls come at a frenetic rate. I wake up in Seoul to missed calls on my cell phone, logged at 4 a.m. my time. She doesn't understand the time difference. I go to work some days to find she's called the *JoongAng*'s Washington bureau, whose staff complains to my supervisor.

I feel exposed. Umma is a problem that I need to cover up.

I call home to try to reason with whichever family member picks up.

"Can you tell her to stop calling?" I plead with my dad. What I really mean is *Can you help protect me?* It doesn't register that I'm asking the man who used to beat me for protection. Appa is my favored parent, deep flaws and all. Through a cold calculus, he is the safer parent.

Our calls always seem to go the same way. Appa picks up. He doesn't say much. It's never a good time for Umma to talk. Away from home, what I'm not seeing is *disorganized speech*, *disordered behavior*, terms a mental health professional might use in a diagnosis that will come too late.

"This is embarrassing me," I say.

Across the line, across the Pacific, Appa sighs. He sounds tired. Business is going badly for him. I wonder if he regrets listening to Umma, who urged him to give up his Presbyterian ministry so they could cash in on construction work during the early-2000s real estate boom.

"Mommy crazy," he replies, pronouncing it like "cray-jee." His thick Korean accent holds on stubbornly, despite his decades of living in the United States.

When Umma calls, I know it's not just because she wants to hear my voice. I picture her mind twisting reality like thick black wires, compelling her to dial whatever numbers might link her to me on the nights her *anxieties*, *delusions*, *hallucinations* come alive. Appa and my sisters can't—or won't—stop her.

I'm home from college on my freshman year winter break. Umma is driving with the car radio tuned to the Korean station. A familiar commercial plays, one of the only ones in English.

A lady's voice says that real estate is the path to the "American dream." Umma pulls into a strip mall dripping with chintzy chinoiserie against cheap plastic signs for businesses. She brings me into an office where she and another middle-aged Korean woman prattle on in a language that has never felt like mine.

At the end of the meeting, Umma tells me to sign a thick stack of documents.

"What is this?" I ask.

The lady is a mortgage loan officer. She speaks English like Umma and Appa, as if her tongue is too thick for her mouth. "Your parents are buying another home, an investment property," she explains. Their credit is too bad to qualify for the mortgage on their own, so by cosigning, I, a college student with a limited credit history, make their home loan application stronger.

Despite the bounced tuition checks and the missed payments, I want to trust them. I don't want to be the haughty, ungrateful daughter that I fear I am. I feel obligated to help. Umma thinks this investment home is her ticket to a better life. It's 2004, and in our McMansion-dotted suburbs, the housing bubble is swelling, fat and tempting to Umma. It looks like living outside our means to me.

I work through the stack of documents, not understanding what I am signing away with the ballpoint pen placed before me.

Hannah Bae.

Hannah Bae.

Hannah Bae.

My parents decide to use my checking account to pay the mortgage. By this point, their financial instability prevents them from opening another account in their own names only. My sisters' finances are in no better shape. I am their only option. My parents plan to find a tenant who will pay rent on the investment house, and that rent will cover the mortgage payments. Simple.

By 2009, the global financial crisis is raging. My parents' tenant often can't make rent. The mortgage payment overdraws *our* checking account. They have already ruined their credit. Now they are ruining mine.

Three years into my life in Seoul, I am doing well for myself. The savings I earn, stashed in Korean banks, tick higher every month.

I don't think about my United States finances while I'm here—those dollars are on ice because I pay for everything in Korean won.

One day, as I rifle through the desk drawer where I keep my unused United States debit and credit cards, I notice that one is expired. *Better request a replacement*, I think as I log into my account.

When the screen loads, I blink in disbelief. There are too many zeros. My card's balance is thousands of dollars higher than it should be.

Have I been hacked? I think, frantically scrolling through the recent transactions.

McDonald's.

Groceries.

Industrial . . . something.

I squint at the screen. I don't recognize any of these charges.

I fire up Skype and call my parents.

"Hel-loh." It's Appa.

I grill him, my stomach knotted, my body barely squeezing out enough air to form words.

"My business . . ." he says. I detect a falter in his voice. "There no work. I can't pay my workers. I need equipment, there no money."

He used my credit card. A replacement already came to my parents' home in the mail, and he opened it and bought himself construction equipment worth thousands of dollars. Then my mom used the card to get groceries. Then my sisters bought McDonald's. And so on.

Does this count as a crime? Is my family a bunch of criminals? The truth seems murky. It is only years later, in therapy, that I can put a name to how I feel in the moment: betrayed. I will learn that what has happened to me is called *financial abuse.*

Appa promises to pay off the credit card, and we hang up.

I confide in my roommate, who gets her parents on the phone. Her father calmly helps me plan how to pull my finances away from my parents' grabbing hands. Gently, he adds, "You need to pay off those credit card charges that they made under your name. They're never going to do it themselves." It's hard to hear the truth. But this is what he's really saying: I have permission to cut my parents off.

I pay off the credit card debt—about ten thousand dollars, equaling more than ten million Korean won—in one painful go. It wipes out my savings account. This is the cost of financial freedom.

A few days later, I dial my parents' number one more time.

"Hel-loh," Appa answers.

"Dad . . ." My voice wobbles as I hunch over my desk in my Seoul apartment. I try to make my voice hard, like quick-dry nail polish. *Hard As Nails*, like the label says. I have to make my heart hard too. "I decided"—I pause, weighing the gravity of my words—"I don't want to talk to you or Mom until you pay me back."

Appa chuckles as he says, "Okeh. Okeh."

I haven't heard his voice since.

The word "caretaking" conjures up feelings of benevolence toward a weak, defenseless being. When I try to remember ways that Umma took care of me when I was young, most of the memories feel like vapor, forgotten.

I do remember being a thumb-sucker. "You are too old for that," Appa says, although I can't remember how old I am. He tries coloring my thumb with my marker, but I'm smart enough to wash it off. Umma takes out a mini bottle of magenta Estée Lauder nail polish from a free-gift-with-purchase package. The cap of the delicate brush gleams gold under the light as she paints my tiny fingernails. I spread my fingers wide, and she shows me how to blow on them to make them dry. Once the polish sets, hard like plastic, it won't wash off. It's so pretty, I don't want it to wash off—and I don't want to suck my thumb anymore either.

In my last years in Seoul, I work for the State Department, in the press office of the United States Embassy. One morning, an email lands in my inbox.

Subject line: *Missing American Overseas.*

It says that a "Hannah Bae" has been reported missing by her mother. The blood rushes to my face as I recognize Umma's name on-screen.

I reply immediately, apologizing to my colleague tasked with this "missing American" report. *That's my mother. She's mentally ill, and this is a false report. Please disregard.*

I feel cold, almost robotic, as I read over my words on-screen. *What kind of person says "please disregard" about her mother?*

It feels absurd, like something out of a Kafka short story, to have my mother report me missing to the State Department when I am *working* for the State Department. This will not be her last false report.

A few months later, I pick up my desk phone at the Embassy.

Umma's voice pierces my eardrums as she launches into her high-pitched rambling.

This isn't the first time she's reached me at work. Through some bureaucratic miscommunication, she's learned that if she calls the Embassy, the switchboard operators will route her to my direct line. It's a crack in the protective shell I've built.

Umma's wailing bores through the seven thousand miles separating us between Korea and Virginia.

The shock always rattles some deep part of me. There's never any warning that it's Umma—the operators' connection appears as an internal number on my end.

I can't make out a word of what she is saying. After six years in Seoul, I speak Korean with conversational fluency, but her disorganized speech, I will learn, is a symptom of schizophrenia.

My veneer of controlled calm shatters. I forget I'm in my cubicle at work, exposed to my coworkers, as I explode.

"STOP CALLING THIS NUMBER," I splutter into my phone. Everyone can hear. "DON'T EVER CALL ME AGAIN. I DON'T WANT TO TALK TO YOU." It is obvious to the quiet, young Korean women working nearby that I am sobbing.

I slam the phone down, as if banging plastic against plastic can release the rage I feel for my mother on the other end of the line.

That is the last time I've spoken to her.

It took thirty-two years for me to learn that Umma and I share a history as unmothered daughters.

Five years after I cut ties with her, I flew from New York, my recently adopted hometown, back to Korea to research my parents' roots. I wondered if I could find a link between the traumas of my generation and those who came before us.

I spent most of my time in Gwangju, my father's ancestral hometown, the site of a brutal 1980 massacre of pro-democracy civilians. On my last day in Korea, back in Seoul, my news assistant and I met at a local government office a stone's throw from the *JoongAng Daily* newsroom. Some of the storefronts had changed, and new skyscrapers streaked across the cerulean sky, but downtown Seoul still felt like home.

I requested a copy of my mother's family registry, then sat on a bench with my assistant, flipping through the pages.

"Who's this?" my assistant asked. On the page where Umma's mother would be, two women's names were listed. Judging by the dates, the first one was Umma's mother.

Umma's father separated from her mother in July of 1963, a few days shy of Umma's eighth birthday. Four months later, on Christmas Eve of 1963, at 11 p.m., her mother was declared dead.

Her name was Jang Jeong-hee. That was the first time I ever learned of her existence.

The other woman listed is the one I've called Grandma my whole life. She married Umma's father three years after his first marriage ended. When my sisters and I were growing up, we almost never visited these grandparents. In the last concrete memory I have with them, we're watching the 1996 Atlanta Olympics on TV.

When I returned home to New York, I brought the family registry to my therapist's office. Together, we studied the pages like tea leaves, trying to find meaning.

"This is a total guess," she ventured, "but I think there is a chance that your maternal grandmother committed suicide. She was abandoned by her husband, who kept her kids. She wouldn't have had many options."

There was only so much we could guess when the documents revealed so little. I wondered what it was like for Umma to lose her mother.

I told my husband everything when I got home. I told my in-laws, then my close friends. I didn't say a word to any of my relatives. I'm afraid to ask how much they know.

Later, after my sisters read some of my writing, they decided to interrogate relatives on the maternal side of our family. *Death by tuberculosis*, they reported back. No one wanted to share much more. I regretted stirring up decades-old grief, a long-buried memory. But still, my heart ached for my mother at age eight, motherless. *Me too, Umma.*

Estrangement doesn't erase the fact that I am my parents' daughter. I recognize my father's athleticism in my rhythmic stride as I run, his love of learning in my pile of library books. I see my mother's jawline when I blend creamy foundation into my skin, her fashion sense in my wardrobe's floral prints, the warm magenta and coral red.

When I picture Umma, she's the most beautiful version of herself, a nineties queen in shoulder pads and shiny Talbots pumps, standing at the front of the church. Her skin, the pride of a Korean woman, gleams pearl-like with the sheen of artfully applied Estée Lauder foundation. Her lips stretch into a perfect pastor's-wife smile. The clarity of her diamond voice cuts through the thick air of the sanctuary. *Remember me this way*, she sings, and I want to listen.

Father Outside

Nick Flynn

A black river flows down the center
of each page

& on either side the banks
are wrapped in snow. My father is ink falling

in tiny blossoms, a bottle
wrapped in a paperbag. I want to believe
that if I get the story right

we will rise, newly formed,

that I will stand over him again
as he sleeps outside under the church halogen
only this time I will know

what to say. It is night &
it's snowing & starlings
fill the trees above us, so many it seems

the leaves sing. I can't see them
until they rise together at some hidden signal

& hold the shape of the tree for a moment
before scattering. I wait for his breath
to lift his blanket

so I know he's alive, letting the story settle

into the shape of this city. Three girls in the park
begin to sing something holy, a song
with a lost room inside it

as their prayerbook comes unglued

& scatters. I'll bend
each finger back, until the bottle

falls, until the bone snaps, save him

by destroying his hands. With the thaw
the river will rise & he will be forced
to higher ground. No one

will have to tell him. From my roof I can see
the East River, it looks blackened with oil

but it's only the light. Even now
my father is asleep somewhere. If I followed

the river north I could still
reach him.

Clearing My Throat

noam keim

My astrologer tells me I will be healing my mother wound
this spring.
My mother whom I have not spoken to in over a decade.
My mother who never spoke the language of our ancestors.
Who made me believe that to be loved meant to relinquish myself.
My astrologer tells me I will be shifting my relationship to home.
Away from the American city where I have lived since I cut ties
with my family in France.

Relax the throat to pronounce the letters that do not exist in the languages you currently speak. The ق and the ح cannot be created in the tightness of a body that carries the guilt of leaving, the guilt of moving, the guilt of learning to speak again in the middle of one's life. Relax the throat, my Arabic teacher repeats over and over. My Arabic teacher doesn't know that my throat was shaped by colonial languages, oppressive structures that carry litanies of apocalypses.

My Arabic teacher doesn't know the stories of family violence, erasure, and destruction that my throat is trying to overcome. She is an employee of the local language school, who knows me as the writer in residence coming from America.

She doesn't know that before there was America, there was France. And before France, my grandparents, Moroccan Jews from Marrakech, colonized the deserts of Palestine. My Arabic teacher doesn't know how much of our culture was lost when my elders migrated, the destructive silence that enveloped every mention of our lineage. She doesn't know about my mother's violence, shaped by the Zionism of her youth. She doesn't know the many paths I have taken to escape the harm caused by my elders. My Arabic teacher doesn't know that in the pronouncing of the ق and the ح, I am trying to heal my mother wound, to complete a cycle, to free myself.

I return to my ancestral homeland of Morocco to write a book. A book about the woman who has newly started to define me when all I wanted was to run away from her grip. How do I make sense of myself when aging brings me closer to her shape? In the widening of my hips and jaw, in the reflection of every mirror, I am brought back to memories of her entering middle age. It is something about my eyes, that in short glimpses look exactly like hers. It horrifies me enough that I feel compelled to explore it in the shape of essays.

In my writing, I explore how ancestral practices of craft can help us make sense of relationships. In Fes, I focus my attention to the practice of rug weaving, the ways threads of cotton and wool become tapestry. I am learning from Amazigh weavers how to sit still on a stool, how to look at my loom and find connection and space. My fingers practice tying and cutting endlessly, and at night I write about what this process feels like in my body, connecting the sensations to French theories of consciousness and perception.

In my quest for ancestry, I meet with a young teacher from an Amazigh community in the south, who tells me about the remnants of Jewish culture around his village. He concludes by saying, "A lot of our Amazigh elders were Jewish," and asks me to show him a picture of my grandmother, with whom I share certain features: the shape of my brows, the edges of my cheeks. "She could be my own grandmother's sister," he exclaims before pulling up his phone, comparing the faces of our elders and smiling to me.

What I want to find in Morocco is a way back to the life of our people, the life my mother pretended had never existed. I spend time absorbing the sounds of the streets, walking endlessly across the city, its markets and parks, to make sense of this country that both defines me and feels impossible to reach. In Morocco, I search for the past that my people have tried to erase in the carved details of the bricks and the lingering inflections of those who surround me. I practice my crumbs of language with every shopkeeper I encounter. Every day on my walks I see storks flying above me, a bird I always understand as an omen—the symbol of my home region in France and the English translation of my mother's name. Here, storks are a familiar sight to all but me.

"What do you call this in Darija?" I ask, pointing at the mound of beets laid on a wooden cart, on the sidewalk of the Ville

Nouvelle of Fes. Youssef, the English teacher guiding me around the city to show me the remnants of the Jewish community, tells me that the small roots are known as "barba."

Barba, boiled and sliced on the small plates of my grandmother's house in Bir al-Sabi. Barba, boiled and sliced or shredded in my home of Mulhouse, too, in my mother's kitchen, where the beet was bought preboiled in the small plastic containers of French supermarkets. In both their mouths, the *r* rolled just like it does in Youssef's.

I, too, try to roll the syllables in my mouth, recognizing the thread of belonging offered to me. The name of a root becomes a time traveling experience inside of the throat of those who made me.

In the middle of my stay in Morocco, continuing to dig into my newfound interest in weaving techniques, I hire a tour guide to take me around the villages of the Middle Atlas region to learn from artisans, away from predatory middlemen and orientalist merchants. I settle on visiting a cooperative of rug makers in the village of Aït Hamza, nestled among olive and cherry orchards a few hours away from the city.

A woman wrapped in pink and blue fabric walks ahead of our car as we approach the house of Ito, a known master weaver. As she hears the car, she turns for a few seconds, and in her aging features I swear I see my grandmother, my mother, myself. Brown eyes, wide cheeks, moon face. A few hours later, after the weaving demonstration and couscous and the makroudha, we leave the house to return to our car when I see another ancestral reminder: a stork, perched alone on the tree, observing our group.

In the city of Fes, I attune to the sounds: the morning salutations exchanged with shopkeepers and strangers, the adhan rising from the minarets, the cries of peddlers calling for passersby to purchase their wares. The sounds resonate in my chest, pounding the memory of families lost. In Morocco, sounds feel like a map toward a past that I am trying to access, a lineage that I was cut from, a familial procession that I interrupted when I left. In the conversations I overhear, I find the sounds of my childhood, sounds whose only meaning is the memory of mornings spent in my grandmother's house. The sounds aren't words to my ears, because I was never allowed to understand them as language. But they perpetually echo inside my chest, unable to be retrieved, since I lack access to the people who could teach me what they mean.

I fall in love in Fes. With the city itself, its medina of tadelakt and cedar, of alleys and shadows. With the echo of French and English and Darija that permeates each conversation. With a Cancer who patiently teaches me the language of my ancestors as we walk along the old Jewish Quarter, under the shadows of large storks crossing the bluest of skies. Small words turn into expression, until I can form small sentences. He teaches me to open my mouth wide, to expel the air. From the confines of my throat, I perform the identity I have been searching for.

On my last night in Morocco, I sit in a sterile hotel room in Casablanca and call the ancestral healer who has been guiding me in connection with the people I can't access. I tell him about the feeling of belonging I experience here. I tell him how bare the sky was on my taxi ride from the medina to the train station, how it is the first time the storks didn't come to meet me. How I understand the omen that is being shared with me. And I ask, "Does that mean that it's time to return to the country of my lineage?" My ancestors, through his voice, tell me, "Only come back to Morocco if you desire, but when you do, do not attempt to live the life we had, do not try to inhabit your wound. Instead, create your own path rooted in joy and discovery."

On a video call, my friend Khadijah tells me that when I tell her goodbye, when I say "b'slama," that I sound like a b'ldia, a villager. We both laugh, as my body expands from the recognition.

A year later, I schedule another appointment with my astrologer.
It is spring again and, in a few weeks, I will return to Fes.
My mother sends me an email, telling me she saw an
interview of me on YouTube,
one that she watched ravenously. She writes "It is
funny how you think you are Moroccan."
I don't answer her email. I never answer her emails.
My Cancer lover tells me that relationships are the
foundation of any belonging, before whispering, "Omri, 7ayati,
kanbghrik bezaf bezaf a lmeghribiya deyali."
With his words, he tells me what my body already
knows. I have made my way back home.

Nobody Owns You: A Flash Sonnet

Erika Krouse

1.

Two weeks before my wedding, my mother disowned me for the last time.

JD and I were hosting a big house party to celebrate our upcoming elopement to Thailand. I had invited all my friends and relatives except for X, the man who had sexually abused me from age four to seven. My mother had never disavowed him. I was trying to love her anyway. But she said she wouldn't come if X wasn't invited. It wouldn't be fun for her unless he was there.

After that, it was the invitations that undid her. Vellum on floral-textured green paper, tied together with a red picot ribbon. My brother said when my relatives received their invitations and asked my mother where she was staying, she was enraged at having to explain her intended absence. She said I had invited the family just to embarrass her. She forbade everyone from attending, speaking to me, or telling me I had been disowned. She said, "Tell her when I die." She said, "Let her wonder."

2.

"Wonderful," I kept saying during our monsoon elopement to Thailand, just JD and me on the beach with red flags ripping in the wind, on a seven-dollar-a-day scooter in the rain, or under a shared umbrella eating soggy orange street chicken. Tossing scraps to stray dogs during our wedding dinner at an outdoor cliffside restaurant, rubberwood tables strewn with mosquito coils.

But when I returned home, everything was the same except I didn't have a mother anymore. Or aunts, uncles, cousins, a sister, barely a brother. They had all obeyed my mother's directives. I was erased.

When people asked how I liked married life, I said, "I don't." Then, at their shocked faces, I said, "It's wonderful" and smiled, like it was all a joke.

3.

This is my second favorite joke: A man is relaxing at home when he hears a knock. When he opens the door, nobody is there. He sees a snail on his stoop and punts it across his yard.

Ten years later, he hears a knock on his door again. When he opens it and looks down, the snail asks, "What was *that* about?"

4.

"Look down and you fall," my gymnastics balance beam coach used to say.

After I was disowned, I thrust my chin up and smiled like a morning show host. Sure, I had just lost my entire family, but did I really have them—want them—to begin with? Nothing had changed; everything was fine.

But my body refused to lie. It broke out in rashes and teenage-esque acne, canker sores, diarrhea, bouts of vomiting. I couldn't stop menstruating in thick clots that left me anemic. Nests of hair collected in my hairbrush, in sinks and shower drains. My skin scaled off; my lips cracked. Blood vessels in my eyes broke from sudden crying jags that left me dehydrated and chapped. At night, I descended into full-body tremors that shook the bed and woke JD.

This is loss, my body said. *You are still losing.* My mind countered, *It's a trade.* But I didn't know if it was a good trade, my family for the truth, my voice for goodbye.

5.

I wrote my mother a goodbye letter. I thought about sending it to her, but I was afraid of what she'd do: burn it, lie about it, read it aloud in a mocking voice, or throw it unread in the trash with the potato peelings and sardine cans. Or, perhaps worst, silently read it and do nothing.

Instead, I loaded the envelope with stamps and sent it to the coldest town on earth, with no return address. In the heart of deepest Siberia, whoever lives at 1 Oymyakon Road received a snow-blurred letter, convoyed for three days on Stalin's Road of Bones. Perhaps they had an English dictionary and looked up the words "daughter," "forever," "goodbye," "I disown you too."

6.

"Nobody owns you," said JD, my friends, and a psychic I paid $350 in exchange for this statement, three coyote yip-howls, and instructions from the beyond on how to take a bath with eggs, milk, and lemon. It helped, but not enough. I still felt my mind quivering, rolling, accelerating downward to a place of no light.

My neurology has always been a house built on quicksand. I cannot tear down the house and rebuild somewhere safe. I'm trapped in here. I can only dance for new footing whenever the floor tilts, acclimate myself to tripping, falling.

7.

Early fall has always been the safest season. No birthdays, no holidays, no noticeably absent phone calls. It's the last season before winter, when my mother used to send gifts like an XXL Miss Piggy T-shirt or a set of coasters that say "Hog's breath is better than no breath at all." And then, after my wedding, nothing.

The number of ways to disown your daughter equals infinity.

One winter evening when I was five or six, I stuck out my tongue at my mother. She pushed me out the door and locked it. Snow covered my ankles, melted and froze against my bare toes. The porch light seared my vision, and the woods behind me were hooded in black. Everything looked serrated, like steel. Inside, my mother was making dinner. She opened the oven, and the heating element glowed. She chopped potatoes on a cutting board, the dull *whack* vibrating through the windowpane. I ended up sitting in the snow, holding my feet. They felt like someone else's feet, blue yellow in the porch light. I fainted in blinks.

My mother finally unlocked the door, opened it. I lay across the doorway before she could change her mind.

8.

"I changed my mind—I don't want to be your mother," my mother said. I was nineteen, calling from my dorm room phone, and I had just told her about X for the third time.

"You can't change your mind," I said. "I'm here."

"I can change my mind," she said. "I just can't change anything else."

What I was to her: Any. Thing. Else.

9.

Anything else?

My sister would ask that frigid question when I hovered at her bedroom door after borrowing a pen. A mass of words muted my mouth, stoppered by need.

Anything else?

This is how I ask my brother about my mother, because I don't know what to call her: "Mom," "your mother," "my former mother." There's no wikiHow for disownment. But if I don't ask about her then, I have to wait another year until I call again on his next birthday.

Anything else?

My mother used to ask that question when I finished throwing up. When I finished my homework, finished cleaning the house. My therapist asked it whenever I said "and stuff." Waitresses, fist on hip. Lovers, peeling themselves away after sex, before sleep overtook them but not me.

I've always said "No," but it's never the real answer.

10.

"The answer is no," she said. "Stay up there until you learn your lesson."

My mother left me at the top of the stairs and clomped down to the first floor to make tea. She was gone a long time; I could hear her, but I couldn't see her. When I tumbled down the stairs, my leg caught between the banister bars and broke. My mother rose from the downstairs couch in two moves—halfway, then standing. She bent to settle her teacup softly in the saucer, the ceramic edges scraping, the sound of high wind. This is one of my first memories.

The doctor told my mother he never saw a twenty-two-month-old with a broken leg before. "He acted like I was a bad mother," my mother said for the next sixteen years, as if I had planned the accident, an ambush from a baby.

11.

My panic attacks are ambushes you can set your watch by. At their worst, I've timed them at eleven attacks per minute, and they continue all day and night, every day and night. It sounds impossible even to me, but I've lived this way my whole life. I can't breathe, my lungs like twin irons. My body jerks. I try to twist out of the attacks to a place where I can trust the air. Panic is not fear. When I'm panicking, I fear nothing and crave death, avoid high places so I don't jump. I don't know why my body is still racked by these paroxysms when the worst has already happened.

Drugs never work, so I take MCT oil, fish oil, magnesium, calcium, NAC, 5-HTP, high-dosage B6, vitamin D. Curcumin, probiotics, ashwagandha, L-theanine, phosphatidylserine, melatonin. Kava tea, chamomile tea, lemon balm tea. I've been on a ketogenic diet for so many years, I can't remember what cake tastes like.

Breathing meditations, aromatherapy, heat therapy, art therapy, play therapy. Swimming, hiking, qigong, fucking yoga. 4-7-8 breathing, box breathing, breathing apps. Ketamine microdoses, EMDR, art therapy, binaural theta wave therapy, bilateral sound therapy. The sound waves snag on my corpus callosum, like rags on rust.

All the therapies act like a lopsided brake, and the inside of my brain aches from the whiplash. The internet says this is impossible, that brains have no nerves. My brain is gaslighting itself; nothing can explain the pain or make the panic stop for long.

12.

It didn't stop and didn't stop, so I told my mother what X was doing to me. I was four. My mother had given birth to my brother a few months before, and the baby was sleeping. She sat in our green-tiled kitchen. Before her was a teacup and saucer from the same set as when I broke my leg—smooth matte brown, so dark it was almost black.

She leaned back. My words had erupted like a gushing gash, but she was calm as she said, "What do you expect me to do about it, Erika?"

Her voice was so cool and logical. My mouth flapped open and shut. My mother returned to her buttered toast and tea. I walked away and beat up my Raggedy Ann doll, played "run away" with my yellow Fisher-Price playhouse, watched Wile E. Coyote sprint off cliff after cliff, puffs of dust signaling his insignificant deaths. I later realized my mother had spoken to me like I was an adult, not her four-year-old daughter, or a daughter at all.

This was the first time she disowned me.

To estrange, to make strange. You're different now—different from your old self, different from anyone else you know. You're expected to carry the shame of your difference alone. Retreat quietly. Pretend any of it was your choice.

13.

I pretended my exile was my choice. Pretended I had chosen integrity over silence. That if I had played along like my siblings, I wouldn't have been cast out.

But this was a lie. I was never going to be anything in that family but the role assigned to me. There could be only one king, one queen, one golden child, one lost child, and a scapegoat to justify it all. Everyone had accepted their place but me.

"Their mistake," JD says, and I agree. If they wanted my silence, they should have given me something to lose. They should have left more behind than the skeleton of a child, arm raised in goodbye.

14.

This is my favorite joke: A skeleton walks into a bar and says, "I'll have a beer and a mop."

I need a mop. Everything slides through me now—joy, devastations, insults, celebrations—snagging on nothing, my insides smooth as polished bone. If I do one hundred therapies per day, I can survive second by second this way, staving off my body and its cellular memories. I can pretend I chose the life I have.

I wonder about my sister and brother, how they feel beneath their smiles and nods, hellos and goodbyes. If keeping the peace gives you peace.

But my mind refuses to change. The answer is no. I'm on my own side now. Anything else would be an ambush on reason. I can't gaslight myself without catching on fire.

My role model is Wile E. Coyote. Always outmaneuvered, always speeding off a cliff, legs cycling, pausing midair for a moment before falling to his death. But the very next scene! He's back again, whole and hungry, with a new plan to catch his dinner. The Road Runner thinks he's dumb, but he's not. He's Wile E. Coyote, Super Genius.

Stop. Look down. Fall.

Begin again.

Author's note: Use of the flash sonnet form was inspired by Sherman Alexie's poem "Tattoo Tears."

Prodigal Daughter

Michelle Dowd

> *A thing is mighty big when time and distance cannot shrink it.*
>
> —ZORA NEALE HURSTON

Mark mesmerized me with his sadness, of a weight and texture so familiar, it almost felt like mine. I told him early on that I would leave, that it's what I do, but he didn't believe me. I don't even know if I meant it, but it seemed like a fair warning.

"You know I can't stay," I said to Mark the first time he took off my shirt. "Even if I love you, even if you think whatever we have is working."

"Have you ever thought that maybe I'm different?" he countered, reaching to unhook my bra strap. I shrugged and arched my back to make it easier on him. I spoke to his softly lit reflection in the car window, opening my breasts to the empty field in front of us, idly curious at the way he fumbled at my back.

"Maybe," I said, "but I don't know if I am."

We hadn't seen each other in twenty years, since we were teenagers swaddled in a cult, and he said he regretted we hadn't been sexual back then, suggesting perhaps we had unfinished business. I didn't argue, since I hadn't even said goodbye back then, when I left everyone I knew at the Field. I didn't tell him that I've never liked goodbyes, not even casual ones, how I've learned to slip away unnoticed, even from parties, searching for escape routes upon arriving, so that when I get that panicky feeling, I know where and how to bolt. I didn't tell him how I wanted this option more than caffeine, alcohol, music, or sleep. I craved it more than coming in tandem, needed it more than I need love.

Mark stayed with my family at the Field longer than I did, but even now, I don't know the terms of his exodus. He was reluctant to talk about it, and I accepted this without complaint. He had never married, never lived with a woman, never had a child or attached to the world through those relatively predictable milestones we call settling down, and eventually I would see in the way he avoided eye contact and the subtle slump of his shoulders that his confidence was a ruse, that he never got over the shunning. Having everyone you've ever known stop speaking to you is a harsh ritual. It gets inside of you like a bad dream and wears down the joints and muscles and sinews of what you think of as your corporeal being until you're not sure where you end and anyone else begins.

Mark emailed me at the college where I taught twenty years after we'd last had contact, but even after so much time had passed, he breathed a brokenness I recognized, and I wanted so badly to heal it, I returned his affection almost immediately. I fingered the fear behind his eyes, a palpable pain that resonated more effectively now than it had when I had last seen him at seventeen. I assured him we wouldn't have to talk about our pasts, that we could pick up as we were, that right now was all that mattered.

Mark still resided in the San Gabriel Valley, which held a basin of memories that yanked to roots I thought were buried beyond recollection. When I drove from the high desert to see him, the view of jacarandas and the smell of eucalyptus assaulted me from the freeway, through the surface streets to his Pasadena condominium, permeating even the pastrami sandwiches we shared at The Hat. Walking through the Huntington gardens on his annual membership pass, and feeding the ducks at the arboretum made me weep in ways he assumed were joy.

There we were, two adults trapped in the ghosts of adolescence, unable to communicate in anything but the present tense. This philosophy works well in meditation or a yoga class, but I hadn't yet discovered those things, and one day, when Mark climbed on top of me, I had no idea who he was.

He no longer felt like the boy I had grown up with, and his weight was cacophonous on my body, like the older brothers who mounted me when I was a little girl.

I felt nauseous and stiffened, turning my head to the side, clenching my eyes shut, while he kept undulating, as if copulating a corpse. When he came with no complaint, slid off, and went to the kitchen for water, I threw up over the edge of the bed.

So I left him, too, via a text message the next morning, and I never explained why.

The Meeting Room floats above a football field, balancing on the base of the scoreboard and two rickety wooden pillars, attached at the rear like a pier. I am seventeen and have known every face in this room since before I knew what knowing meant. I was born and raised here, in a hollowed-out former city dump, burrowed into the end of a cul-de-sac, now forged into a basin of athletic fields, a scoreboard tower, and a clubroom we call a church. Each member of this Council of Elders has belonged to this community since before my mother was born. She was the first daughter of our Leader, whom we all call "Grandpa," and she will never leave.

I've lived in this community since I was born, with my entire extended family, several of whom are now Elders in this council, but I don't want to stay here forever. I have petitioned to leave our faith community to go to college, and they have called me into this room to change my mind.

Born here, into this Field Family, I spiritually signed a "commitment for life" form at birth, and the Council interprets this as legally binding. I don't comprehend the distinction between the Field's version of communal law versus state or federal judicial systems, but I tell them I will come back when I am done with my education, that I will sign in blood to devote myself to the Field, all of whom are my clan, and I genuinely believe this can happen. They have indoctrinated me into a way of thinking that has kept me from contact with Outsiders, and I believe I can keep a significant part of myself separate from those Outsiders forever.

"We are all disposable," Dad says, "paper cups worth only what we are filled with. Fill yourself with the Holy Spirit of the Lord our God, and you will have value and purpose."

They have taught me that if I leave, I will be empty, like a hand that doesn't welcome the spirit of the dove, a dove that alights but once. When that dove flies away, it will never offer itself again, because straight is the gate, and narrow is the way, and only a very few will ever find it.

I listen, but since women are to be seen and not heard, I don't inform them that they're mixing metaphors, or that when they're starving, birds will come back to a hand for food, even if they sense danger.

My mother has taught me a lot about birds, but she isn't here to correct their analogies and wouldn't, even if she were. Women aren't welcome in this Council, except to receive discipline or serve as a receptacle to a man's seed. Mother avoids the former and has had too many children from the latter, so she hides on a mountain, as much as she can, learning how to prepare us all to survive the apocalypse.

My mother knows things these men don't know, but she'll never tell them that. She cherishes wild birds and rodents and all things that grow on God's green earth, but she doesn't cherish me. Attachment would destroy her.

Grandpa loves to talk about how Jesus required his disciples to leave their families to follow him, and my mother wants to make her father proud. When we were little, she told us the story about Abraham being called to sacrifice his son Isaac on an altar, how he hiked up a mountain with a sword in his hands and drew it on his own son. Grandpa says all his followers must be prepared to kill their children if they're asked to.

She protects herself from disobedience by refusing to touch us, so she can have the resolve to act on the order of God when he inevitably asks her to kill us.

Like migrating birds, my mother knows how to move in the dark without a flashlight. She can navigate without a map and can go long swaths of time without food or companionship. She knows what plants you can forage and she can cook a meal from those plants and she can decorate a table with a natural centerpiece she made herself, more beautiful than anything in this room.

As I stand in front of the Elders, I wish I were on the mountain, foraging for seeds. And I wonder if my mother thrives in the natural world in spite of her upbringing at the Field or because of it.

I have been raised in the Field's doctrine, so I'm not supposed to respect the work women do or question why we keep ourselves small. I know that we are unlike Amish communities in an essential way: the Field does not welcome back wanderers, because God is capricious, because the Lord our God is a jealous God, and he will not tolerate the vain worship of golden idols.

Sometimes I think God is jealous of women. I mean, it's a strange thing to put a tree in a garden just to tempt someone with the enticement of knowledge. God must have created Eve with more curiosity than Adam, or she wouldn't have been the one to eat the fruit.

I'm not supposed to want knowledge either, but how can I be anything other than who I am? Born and raised here in a world of men, I may have stayed small if my mother hadn't been so uncageable, if she hadn't been perpetually curious, if she hadn't run toward trees the way Eve did. If I hadn't witnessed her find what she needs outside of the Field's programming, in a way even Grandpa doesn't see, I might believe women are naturally subservient.

When we moved to the mountain to lead God's army, our mother would pile us into a World War II Jeep, a rugged army-green relic left on the property, in which she would traipse us over the hills into territory she had not yet labeled or conquered. She learned about God through the flora and fauna while we roamed wild, foraging for plants and practicing our survival skills, should the apocalypse rain down upon us.

Last year, when Grandpa died of a heart attack, I still believed he was God's son, and patiently, day after day, I watched the sky for signs. I waited for the sun to grow dark, the moon to turn blood red, for war to descend upon us, for the blood to rise up to the horses' bridles. They said that an angel took him, and I thought it was the truth, that his bedside had lit up, "and lo, the angel of the Lord was round about them," and I was surprised the staff hadn't been killed for seeing the backside of God.

Yet here I am, in a world that hasn't ended, stuck in an abated apocalypse that has left me hanging in perpetual childhood, disappointed, disillusioned, and discredited.

I sit here in this Council next to Dad, Grandpa's son-in-law, who has the authority to call the meeting to order with the formal dialect he practices at home. "Brethren, you know straight is the gate, and narrow is the way which leadeth unto life, and few there be that find it."

The members grunt their assent. I try to breathe evenly and inaudibly. Every person in this room has known me since I was in my mother's belly, but they speak of me as if I'm persecuting them with my insubordination.

I listen as they continue to pontificate.

"What message will this send?"

"If she returns, who else might she lead astray? What sort of precedent would this set? In these dark times, it's not possible to stay true to the path of righteousness while dwelling in the Devil's kingdom."

"Who does she think she is?"

I don't know who I am without them and will have to leave to find out. But I would wrestle a flaming angel for their blessing.

I take my on-again, off-again boyfriend Chad up to the mountain where my mother used to forage. We climb over a trespassing gate, and I point toward a house the Field built, now inhabited by a man I used to call my older brother, before he felt me up on a ski lift when I was sixteen. We don't see any signs of him but continue onto the upper road uninterrupted, up the narrow trail to an old chapel, where I show Chad how we used to put on the armor of God to protect us from the temptations of the Outside world, and then I tug him up a hill off trail, up to a paved road that seems to have sprung up from nowhere. I tell him how, as a child, I had looked at that road with longing, wondering if I would ever know where it leads.

I point out a lodgepole pine, a tree ubiquitous since the 1986 fire, and I explain to him how you can peel away the outer bark and strip off noodles of the inner bark and eat them raw. I rub my hand along the outside of the tree to show him where the best place to start would be, if we need it. My hand is sticky from the sap, so I roll it between my fingers into a little ball. "You can eat this pitch when your throat is sore from thirst."

Chad looks at me like I'm speaking a foreign language and shrugs. "Seems like a fun way to grow up."

I put a leaf in my mouth and chew it, thinking how lucky I am he'll never know me well enough to hurt me.

"Are you sure that's safe?" he asks.

"I'm sure," I say. "Yerba santa is listed in the 1894 US Pharmacopeia as an official remedy for coughs, pneumonia, and bronchitis."

"How do you know?" he asks.

"I know a lot of things that aren't particularly useful."

Chad looks bored and walks down the hill toward the car without glancing back, and I feel small, like folded laundry set in a basket.

I watch him go, relieved I don't need him. I can survive in the desert, flatlands, wetlands, or forest because I know how to forage from trees, brush, and weeds. I know how to find the sustenance buried everywhere, in lodgepole, Coulter, and Jeffrey pine, in yerba santa, rosehip, nettles, elderberry, prickly pear, dandelions, and more. I can survive in any landscape, without human touch.

Soon I will leave Chad, asleep in his bed, with only a note on the table.

Dad quotes scripture and gesticulates bombastically. The Council has denied my request to leave. I lose track of the argument and the approach, consumed by a rising nausea threatening to erupt in projectile vomit. I excuse myself with a mumbled excuse, my hand wrapped around my belly. The door isn't even closed behind me when I begin retching in waves on the floating stairs, my head bowed in shame so heavy, the Field below spins like a vortex. I clench the rail to combat the vertigo, but my hands are slippery from the bile.

Leaving doesn't feel like a choice as much as an inevitability. I don't know how to go back in, so I shuffle down the stairs and walk across the Field, out the mouth of the cul-de-sac, all the way up to Ralphs grocery, where I use their pay phone to call the admissions officer.

Not missing anyone will become my only goal, the closest I can get to freedom.

My on-again, off-again boyfriend Dave puts out his hand, and a bird sweeps in, nabbing the peanut from his palm. He smiles and tells me he's been coaxing this bluebird into a relationship with him ever since he moved into this former monastery he's converting into a home he will live in for the rest of his days.

I tell him that it's a Steller's jay, and he looks at me. "Are you sure? You barely saw it."

"I'm sure," I say.

Dave seems surprised. He pulls out a book and he shows me pictures of birds that are blue. I turn to the entry on the Steller's jay and read him the caption.

"You're right," he says. "How did you know?"

I tell him I know a lot of useless things—he will soon be one of them.

As my mother lay dying, I curled up on her urine-soaked hospice mattress, holding her hand as she struggled to breathe. I lifted my puppy up onto her belly, and I lay beside the two of them, snuggling the puppy as my mother labored to die.

My mother was once a mountain woman who spoke dog, so the nurse doesn't question me. The puppy and I are on the bed, our bodies draped across my mother's belly, as she draws her last breath.

When my mother was diagnosed with pulmonary fibrosis and her lungs were stiffening, her doctor recommended she find a yoga teacher to work with her on her breathing. She had stayed at the Field with my father and never forgave me for leaving, but when she emailed to tell me the news, I told her I would come over. Even though she hadn't acknowledged my life since the day I left and we had never made peace with that rupture, I put her right hand on her belly and her left hand on her heart and I maneuvered her through several body positions, breath sequences, and relaxation techniques. She didn't make eye contact with me, but she hesitantly followed my instructions.

I was perplexed by the hunger in my body, sitting so close to her on a yoga mat. I had thought I might be angry, but all I felt was famished for all the years we had lost and all that lay unspoken between us. I thought I was over the shunning, but I was a child who had fallen into a well and the cavern inside was dark and endless. I considered telling her this, but the chasm felt like the Grand Canyon, and I had no way to cross it.

When I reached to hug her goodbye, she stiffened. Physical affection wasn't something she provided when we were children, and I clearly yearned for what she couldn't bestow.

After her death, the puppy and I made our way up to the mountain to plant her ashes with a sapling near a fallen tree, desiccating for decades.

On the way back, we stopped by the Wrightwood museum. A docent in her early seventies introduced herself as Barbara and said I could look around.

When I spent an inordinate amount of time looking at a photo of the ranger station, she asked me if I knew Mrs. Dowd, who used to give talks there. "She was quite the naturalist. Legendary. You'd remember her if you met her. Smart as a whip, that one."

I was tempted to lie, but I've stopped running from what formed me, so I nodded and told her that was my mom.

"Well, Lord have mercy, what a day. Mrs. Dowd is your God-given mother? She was a spitfire, that one. More energy than I ever seen in a woman, and Lord, what a whirlwind of knowledge she had in her, God bless her." She glances at me to see how

I'm taking this, then continues, "How is your mama these days, love?"

"She's good," I said, not sure how to tell her she was no longer living.

Like my mother, I speak dog.

"What a trip," Barbara exclaimed, "to think you were up the hill the whole time. What a trip! Worked with your mama for years. Never thought she had children. Never would have guessed."

I dismissed myself to get the puppy some water, which I let overflow from the metal bowl onto the rocky soil, where it formed foamy puddles that went nowhere. I picked some yerba santa and put it into my pocket, in case I was thirsty later.

I looked out over the landscape, noticing the curves of the hillside, envisioning the rippling water in the basin of the Devil's Punchbowl and the copious tumbling and transparent waterfalls that flow into it. The stark colors of the sun on the rock formations radiated and swirled and dominated the landscape. Nothing else has ever been as rich or robust or permeating, and nothing I have encountered since runs that deep.

When I burrowed into my mother's dying body, soft with the scent of the pack, whatever roles we played with one another looped around like a Möbius strip. She showed me the freedom of unattachment. And gave me the ability to detach from everyone, except her.

My mother was my first country, the first place I ever lived. I learned survival skills and the intelligence of nature from her, and I've clung to those even when I've lost the ability to stay connected to other intimacies. I have sat quietly on many mountains, listening to the teeming sounds of layers of life, feeling perfectly at home.

The puppy and I climbed into my car and left the museum without saying goodbye. When I glanced at my reflection in the rearview mirror, I thought I saw my mother looking back at me.

We survive in the only ways we know how.

A few miles down the mountain, I turned around to see if I could catch her watching, but the desert landscape was barren, just like when I left my family the first time. I reached into my pocket for the yerba santa and put a few leaves into my dry mouth to ward off the imminent thirst. The rest, I tossed out into the wind, a futile bid for my mother's love.

Water Is Thicker

Alyson Shelton

I'm eight years old, on this picture postcard of a summer afternoon in sunny SoCal. I drift toward the bottom of the silty bay, exhaling, imagining air bubbles floating upward and popping when they hit the surface. I remain even as my exhalation runs its course. Even as I feel my chest tighten from the lack of oxygen.

But I know exactly how far I've sunk. I'm ninety-nine percent certain I'm not going to die.

I take a beat longer. Ninety-eight percent.

And then I rise, gulping down the air and wiping my eyes as my legs tread water.

I choose this breathlessness. I push myself to my limits and beyond regularly. I'm in training. Always in training. To be a part of this family is the most extreme sport I know.

My brothers, "The Boys," as they are often called, are numerous and older and half mine. "Half" hits home like a gut punch when Michael, the second oldest, falls from a cliff and dies when I am ten.

At Michael's makeshift wake, weaving through relatives stinking of beer and laughing so loud I feel I must hide my tears, I hear from my aunt and cousins:

"You shouldn't be that sad. He's only your half brother. You have three more."

As if they are interchangeable. As if he is not my favorite. As if he is not the only one to stand up to our oldest brother, Paul, to show me a way to escape. As if my body understands halves. All it understands is:

He was mine. And now he is gone. Don't be next. Train harder.

After Michael's death, we settle into a heightened version of ourselves. We smile. A lot. Too much. In this Stepford neighborhood, no one appears to notice our unsettling transformation into a united team, but I do. When did we all become so aggressively happy? When did we all start wearing pastel uniforms, tossing our arms over each other's shoulders, and smiling for cameras only we can imagine?

It's the summer of 1984 and the Los Angeles Olympics. The gymnast Mary Lou Retton is America's sweetheart, the strongest girl I've ever seen anyone love. I am obsessed. I drown myself in Olympics knowledge, in a sea of factoids, to beat my brothers in Trivial Pursuit, yes, but also to know—because knowledge in our never-ending familial contest will be my gold-medal event. I am still young enough to believe there are "right" answers, and I intend to find them.

My first memory, I uncover much later. In it, I am not years but months old.

I gasp. I gag. I can't breathe.

I remember Paul's shaggy hair. The sound of the teeth of his zipper unlocking. The aroma of sweat and marijuana mingling.

And his laughter.

Paul is my father's clear favorite. Handsome and charming and dangerous. More drugs (that he both deals and ingests) and girls than he can handle. I find ways to survive his cruelty, which can flash, flooding me without warning. I learn to hold my breath when pulled under.

At age twenty-eight, he reacts to Michael's death with a dizzying sea change. Suddenly he dates only one girl at a time, whose name we actually learn. She is more than a flavor of the month; she is Jill. He tries, at this very late date, to play the role of a "good" guy, the team captain. He's finally fulfilling my father's prophecy that rings in all our ears when we try to point out Paul's addiction or abuse:

"He'll grow out of it."

Less than two years before, Paul had been nursing a gunshot wound to his face, from a "work-related incident," at our dining room table. And now he's engaged.

If I stand in front of the metal filing cabinet of my mind and I pull out the top drawer, labeled *Family Trauma*, Paul's folder bulges and overflows. There is so much, too much, I can't even begin to understand—or name—it all, like at the age of thirteen when I stand, looking out at the saccharine-sweet Hawaiian sunset, the pinks and oranges appalling in their thirst to be seen, and feel Paul's hand on my ass, working its way inside my thigh, his breath on my neck, warm, warmer than the tropical air.

"Whoa, I thought you were Jill." His thirty-year-old bride-to-be.

I train to accept this kind of "mistake." It's not his first, and he's not the only man in my family to make one with me.

I train to focus my senses elsewhere. I retreat silently when I stumble on him freebasing coke. I listen to the ocean waves crashing on the night shore instead of his drunken fistfight outside my window.

I train. Until I can't anymore.

People always want to know:

"Why did you stop talking to him?"

It's not one thing. Not one ass grab. Not one drug deal or gunshot wound. Not one time pinning me down till I can't breathe. Not the assault or threat of assault or belittling. Not the fear, the constant fear, when I'm in his presence, no, no, it's not the one thing.

For years, I practice different answers, waiting for a look of recognition on the listener's face. A face that says:

"I get it. You had no choice."

But no matter how many solutions I offer to the problem of "Why, why did you stop talking to him?" I never receive the acceptance I desire. At best, I get a facsimile. People who care for me and want to take my word for it but wonder if I couldn't have given him "just one more chance." And at worst, I face that time-worn phrase, uttered too often and sometimes spit out venomously by extended family or people I thought were my friends:

"Blood is thicker than water."

My first memory of Paul. His laughter and my tiny self struggling to breathe, it (re)materializes in my brain, on spring break when I am seventeen, when another boy named Paul violates me. He ignores pleas, my tears, the word "No." His words on repeat:

"Just relax. Chill. Don't be a bitch about it."

I don't relax. I don't use my physical strength to fight back—which fills me with shame for years. But I do get out. I do survive.

For me, that's the beginning of the end of my nuclear family. Of relentlessly proving my worth with accolades. Of trying to numb my rage by sharpening myself to perfection. I grasp at the until-now-veiled truth: no grade, no medal, no body size will force them to consider me. I've believed that with enough dedication I would eventually ace their challenges and gain acceptance. But our ideas of winning stand in stark opposition. I want to be seen, and they want to render me invisible.

My brother Paul hurts me in countless ways, but my recovered memory of his assault shifts everything. I can no longer accept the excuses or the blame for his abuse. The only way to know myself is to cut him out of my life. And so I do.

I don't have the word "estrangement" in 1991, at age seventeen, when I first begin to drift away from my family. Or in 1996, after a horrific Thanksgiving visit from my father, when I finally confront him, begging him to believe me about Paul, and he says:

"Don't make me choose. You know I'll choose him."

I do know. But I believe he will lie. The way he says it out loud, without pause, shakes me.

After my father flies home, I sit in my apartment, alone on my futon couch, and tremble in fear. Something must change. That night, instead of sleeping, I pick up my pen and write a letter to my father and two half brothers.

"Don't contact me unless you go to therapy. Don't write or call until you can admit what you've done."

They don't call or write. There is no struggle on their end, not that I can see. The anticlimax of it all unmoors me.

And yet, there is struggle. Mine. All these years later, I know my strength. I push myself to do what, on some days, feels impossible. To continue. To unpeel the years, the sticky and tentacled familial relationships. To forgo my father's wealth and the promise of my inheritance. To walk away wounded but alive.

After I send the letter, I settle myself into one scalding hot bath after another.

I let the water hold me while I allow previously dangerous thoughts to bubble to the surface of my consciousness:

"Who am I?"

I am twenty-two and wonder:

"What do I like?"

"Am I a selfish bitch?"

"Am I impossible to love?"

And the answer is "yes." That's what I've been my whole life; one letter can't change all that.

I don't stop training for survival, but the letter changes the flow of my days. I don't weigh whether I should call or write, whether I should stay updated on all things pro sports so I can keep the conversation moving with scores and trades. I stop windsurfing, snow skiing, and scuba diving. I can't afford it anymore. And I don't care. I no longer need to dive to the bottom of the tropical ocean or shush down a powder-covered mountain to pretend we have something in common.

I begin to prioritize not how things look to the outside world but how they feel to me. I move apartments and don't share my address with my family. My new phone number is unlisted. I live near the ocean again after years away. I kick under the surface, tap the bottom, and rocket toward the blue sky. I bob over waves, eyeing the horizon, and consider:

"What do I want?"

I piece it together. And not in a way that feels linear or neat or perfect. I fumble. I speak my mind more and apologize less for taking up space in the world. I lose my shit. I can't sit in a warm car with the windows rolled up or let anyone touch my neck, ever. I sob uncontrollably—in my apartment elevator, at the end credits of the movie *Blow*, in the shower, staring out at the Pacific Ocean.

And emotion drains from my body when confronted with a safe harbor—unconditional love from the man I adore, new in my life. When he holds me, questions crisscross my brain in a spirited game of racquetball:

"But what does he *really* want?"

"Why would he love *me*?"

And most importantly,

"What is this going to *cost* me?"

I try to believe his answers like "Nothing. I just want to be here with you" are true.

I let him sit with me during the end credits. When it is just the two of us, I slow my panicked breathing, wipe my eyes with the heel of my palm, and try to explain what I'm still trying to untangle: My brother hurt me, and yes, intellectually, I know he'll never murder me, but my body is not so sure. My beloved listens, doesn't tell me I'm acting crazy, and never mentions blood or water.

I learn to navigate this world on my own terms. I start to say "no" more often. I build something. On a faulty as hell foundation, but I build it anyway because I start to believe, when I ask myself the question:

"Who am I?"

that the answer is not:

"A total, irredeemable piece of shit."

And that is a life-changing revelation.

I build a whole life, the one I want, complete with a safe home, a caring husband, children whom I cherish, and friends who make me laugh and who understand my choices, without judgment.

I know now, with absolute certainty, that I deserve a life without terror. It was him or me. And I chose me.

I no longer live in fear of the floodwaters of his abuse. In this world I fashioned from my choices, I am sometimes at sea. But I am the vessel, the ocean, and the weather.

ESTR NGEMENT

Gabriela Denise Frank

> *The absence of a sign is always the sign of an absence.*
>
> —WALTER MOTTE

When, from the beginning, something is missing, could it be termed "loss"? How does one put into words things she doesn't know? How to describe lifelong deficiency to those who've only experienced the thing's ever-presence? One must invent new methods to convey her every position, whether enormous or diminutive. This is intensive, never-ending work.

To wit: If one word is nonexistent in your lexicon yet key to the world's discourse, you must modify your responses to express yourself effectively. It's not everyone else's problem but yours—your experience is the "divergent" one. This impediment will undergird your choices in expression, from public speeches to discussions to simple questions.

To exist within society, then, requires more diligence by the experiencer of deficits, not those who enjoy effortless existence. The work of spoon-feeding digestible concepts is thus borne by the dispossessed. Tell me, if you've only known the circuitous linguistic route since birth, why is the burden of describing something, for which you hold no words, on *you*?

Here's the eerie thing: In going unspoken, unvoiced terms

collect otherworldly strength for, despite the world's obsession with possessions, life is formed not exclusively of solids but of voids. Think mesh, filigree, screen—think holes designed to weep. One purpose of voids is conduction. Holes provide courses through the incomprehensible, ergo hollows in elocution provide openings for the unexpected to occur in token disclosures.

Note: Some listeners will be put off by the unwieldy complexity of your speech. Before voicing opinions, you (re)compose whole sentences in your mind, shifting diction or order, wondering if people will get it. Sometimes (often) they won't. Yet your "limited" perspective yields insights buried within the "complete" lexicon, which most people infrequently flex. Your speech, peppered with flowery digressions, edges on perplexing, but multitudinous possibilities reside within your serpentine constructions.

Due to this skewed viewpoint, you've come to define love differently from most. For you, it's rooted in mother, then withers quickly. The other person dwelling in your childhood home? Well, this person yelled. His fuse burned quick. He stunk of engine grit; he wore uniforms. When pushed beyond his limit, he swore, he tickled you till you cried, he hit. His notions of women were regressive (TLDR: virgin/whore), hence your girlhood construction of self could be described in terms of self-disgust, resentment, or mistrust of the feminine (see: misogynistic).

When your mother died, she deserted you.

To reword: The person you loved most dumped you with *him*.

Bereft of her tenderness, you grew up remote, opportunistic, selfish—just like he predicted. You were forced to redefine love, self-worth, kin. When you turned eighteen, you fled home one morning while the uniformed person worked. On discovering your perfidy, he swore retribution; he disowned you, then you disowned him.

Ever since, when something resembling security emerges, you pounce. When things get rocky, you split. You never fight—the quickest end to conflict is simply to lose—you weep discreetly, then bolt or ghost. This is why the inclusion missing from your youth continues to elude you. You've wed (twice), but belonging is—still—nowhere to be found. Look, some people luck out. They grow up with gentle men, which seems to fix everything, but it's not your story. It's merely how it goes. There's no indignity to it.

Truth is, there's no home protected from loss, including ones helmed by gentle men. There's no dodging sickness or demise, not even in close-knit gene pools where people phone often. Worth noting: You've done difficult work, kiddo. Word by word, you've woven your spooky little existence from the few obscure terms you could spell. While your rules of composition require more energy, you've never shirked the responsibility to define things for yourself, nor did you renounce society, not even when you grew tired of deciphering your "odd" terms for others' comprehension.

Though you don't converse (you lost his number), periodic reports of the uniformed person zip over the wire. He continues to tend those bottomless wells of bile without owning up to his role in self-induced exile—three wives down, none to go—so, it seems, you chose right.

The recompense of quitting took its sweet time.

The gift of turning fifty is knowing you wouldn't shift one single, shitty thing, despite his toll on your life. There's no meting injury from cure—lose one, thence goes the other—still, it's surprising to discover you no longer hold the old grudge. The freight of hostility grew so ponderous, it seems you set it down, but you're unsure when or where. One night, it's simply missing. It hits with sheer force: You're his offspring but no longer his child.

Though it's no competition, you find yourself out in front of your normie friends who begin to collide with crises in midlife. You know there's no "success," no idyllic existence, no living without debility or sickness. Impediment seizes everyone. Yours just turned up sooner.

Suffering doesn't connote deservedness of torment, nor is it possible to elude strife by being "good." Don't confuse nosedives with punishment—people's wings melt—no life is impervious to grief, loneliness, doubt. I beg you, uncouple wrong from different, foundling from loser. Consider how *other* is used to construct or buttress *we*.

Remember: Your diversions from orthodoxy don't signify schism—your divergence is gorgeous. You know it's bogus to think one method of expression is the sole or "correct" one. Besides, your weird upbringing yields fortuitous opportunities for connection with people you might otherwise overlook.

Confession time?

For much of my life, I've shielded people from truths I couldn't utter: I grew up with holes in my household, so I pretended to be tough while secretly desiring wholeness. It felt too perilous to express my distress—besides, no one could cure foregone deficits—so I spoke of my hurt in circles (like this), enduring more bruises with every retelling. The few who did receive the unpolished story of my disownment shied from the knowledge or tried to fix me. (Come on. Like I didn't try to fix myself.) Result? Silence seemed the better policy, if only to prevent people's meddlesome pity or my further injury.

The problem is, shielding one's genuine self requires immense energy-sucking upkeep, which is impossible to support endlessly. While clever linguistic tricks do yield surprising insights, they divert focus from the imperfect person hiding under the guise of convincing fictions. The trouble resides in the dichotomy between the felicitous disguise versus the wounded soul stifled behind it. You see, the self's holes won't mend on their own. To fix the rifts, you must surrender your costume, debride your injuries, then simmer your regrets with unprecedented loving-kindness. Remember: Genetics don't secure fidelity, require duty, nor incur debt. Someone's ire is more often their shit, not yours.

To reword, it registered over time: The uniformed person from my youth would dwell in me rent-free if I let him. Some thoughts I inherited, others I forged, but I needed to decide which to dump or keep. In the light of evolved perspectives, my spleen emptied its sluice: If love didn't exist, love couldn't be lost. No tie forged, none to sever—none to mourn.

I poured this golden elixir into the fissures splitting my core, gilding the hurt bright. Though the fluid filled the holes, the wounds never crusted closed. It sunk in: For the benefic effect to persist, the medicine must pour continuously through the injuries. The process of letting go doesn't occur just once—you never stop concocting the potion, nor pouring it through—you let go over, then over, then over.

The body is mostly formed of voids, not cells or electrons but the territory between. Everyone is composed of ruptures. (Hint: The secret to "winning" isn't control but flow.) See for yourself. Stop—get quiet. Listen to the ghostly music singing in your blood. Do you perceive the numinous thrum surging through your veins? You don't need words to describe this commodious energy, this holiness (get it?)—this is life, *your* life, you're living it now, this very moment, the incongruous notes, the off-key jingles, the gritty countermelodies you've tried to smooth over—quit muffling them! Belt out the erroneous chorus! See how your weirdness tunes the sufficient into the incredible?

Extend your fingers—or try. Mine sit outstretched, inviting yours. Feel how we're connected by remoteness, joined by the emptiness between us?

If you get stuck, try letting go of the ossified story you think you know. Trust me, I get it. To expose your essence to the cold, cruel world is to risk violence to your tender core, but (irony's twist) to hide your true self is to not truly live. The choice, in the end, is yours.

Author's note: This essay is a lipogram, a literary constraint utilized by the Oulipo. A lipogram is writing that excludes one or more letters. According to the writer Georges Perec, the word comes from the Greek leipo *("I leave"). This piece leaves out words that contain the letter* A, *an exercise in writing around what's estranged for me:* father, dad, *and* family.

Episodic Tremor and Slip

Lorne Daniel

We learn geology the morning after the earthquake.
—RALPH WALDO EMERSON

1. We Step In

There is no place to start with the mess.
Clothes crumpled, sills stained, grime
on every surface, flat
and vertical. Stench. Blinds down. A cat.
There sits our son, sullen and hunched, head
clamped under headphones. We can no longer start
from hope, we can only approach, sit
in our responsibility and listen when he rants
about landlords, employers, multi-fucking-national
corporations. The great forces
that push him around.

He is 27 and will go nowhere with us, will not travel
this territory, will not reason and accommodate. The place shakes
with his explosions, his booming. Plates rattle, cleavers tremble
and—hearts jumping—we are in full retreat again.

We live in retreat, making plans
for the wrong emergency. Prepare

for what has passed. There is always hope,
friends say. Friends didn't see that basement
suite we rented for him the fall we hoped
he could go back, finish a high school course.
The landlord calls. We step in
and here's a window screen, flimsy
frame wobbling, mesh cut out. Knife blades
scorched into enamel, the kitchen range stripped
down to bare burners. Someone needed to get closer to the flame.

Soon he will sell his dead car for less than he owes, fly
to the east coast, where he knows
no one, and over time we will
locate him, go, sit again. Listen.

I don't want to go on.

2. Small Matters

Another job lost five weeks ago, no biggie,
he says, didn't want to upset us, scraping up
rough, unready words now
through the smoked-out booze-burnt throat
and—wait for it—there's the matter
of rent. When I phone his grandmother
I mention neither. Such are the ways
we believe we lift ourselves above the common
mantle of our lives. Little tricks.

Remember, as a kid, on a perfect summer day,
when a push suddenly sent you skidding
down a slope, how gravel embeds

in the darkened skin of your knees? Earth's
grit in your blood. And you jump
back up, bite your tongue ever so gently? Substitute
the small hurt for the other one.

3. Plan B

We always had a Plan B, except Plan B never worked
any more than Plan A, and all subsequent plans
became named Plan B, over and over, so really
we should have been numbering them B1, B2, B3.
Where would we be now? B52? The bomber or the retro
rockers? Shrug. Whatever. Football. Hockey. Piano.
Judo. Katimavik. We always knew what needed to happen.
(Training? Rehab?) But here we are. Not knowing. Reduced.

4. Calls from Across the Continent

I'm on a bike ride, or in a distant airport, or at a dinner, or
the wedding of a niece. His number comes up.
Hello ugggh I'm dying
I tilt the phone away from my ear
when the dry heaves begin, having learned.
He can't keep water down. Doesn't want a cab
or ambulance to take him to care.
They don't do anything for me blaaaagh dying

When did you start drinking?
This time, I mean. How many
hours, litres? How recently
did you stop? Did you stop? Look,
what can I do?
You can't do anything

Every few hours, his thumb pushes
our speed dial as if to deliver a fix.
Water, I say. Hospital, I offer. Detox. Water.
My words an intravenous drip of sorts.
        blaaa—ugh

I sleep. At 3 a.m. another call, and he
is ready, he says.
        Call an ambulance. Call.

5. On Alert

He agrees to fly west, perch near us,
here on the Juan de Fuca fault. *Makes
no difference to me.* Does detox. Gets clean.
Goes to work, hauling his battered case
of knives from one kitchen to another. High-end, then
the pubs and family grills, then whoever will take him.
Another eviction, furniture abandoned
on the lawn of a kind and weary landlady. We take in
his cat. Clean her up, a cute lion
cut. The cat unimpressed.
One morning she stands alert, ignoring
us and her food. Staring, staring at
nothing, unmoving. Must be sick. Later
in the day, news of a 4.7 quake we never felt,
80 kilometres offshore. Right at the time
we put her food down. Oh, what we miss.

Mother's Day

Cassandra Lewis

It's Mother's Day again. My husband, daughter, and I are about to meet my stepmom and dad for brunch. My eight-year-old asks from the back seat, "Are you going to call her 'Mom' this time?" Variations of this conversation have occurred since my daughter was three, when she first asked about my "other mommy," the grandmother she has never met. I was caught off guard then and every time she raises the issue. My journalist father instilled in me the belief that honesty is essential no matter what. But being left under the supervision of my unstable mother while he prioritized his work taught me that safety is also important.

There is no child-appropriate way to describe abuse and the necessity of cutting family ties. In children's books and movies, estrangement is rarely portrayed as the resolution for achieving survival. Instead, it is a temporary mistake or a problem to be solved through reunification.

The only children's story that remotely resembles my relationship to my biological mother is Margaret Wise Brown's *The Runaway Bunny*, an adorably illustrated tale about a young bunny who wants to run away but his mother tells him, "If you run away, I will run after you." By the time I reached thirty-five and became a mother, I'd lived in twenty-four homes, having moved frequently as a child due to the erratic whims of my mother. And later as an adult, I continued this familiar pattern of always being on the run. I spent most of my adult life hiding from my troubled mother, who has been in and out of jails and prisons for stalking.

Mother's Day used to invite a familiar fog of dread, as well as a phantom pain in my lower back, one that conjured the memory of my mother literally kicking me out of her house when I was fourteen. I'd just changed schools again, this time as a freshman, and had been out sick with mono. My parents had recently separated, and my father's apartment barely had any furniture, not even a television, but I preferred to recover there instead of my mother's house, where her moods were unpredictable. Knowing how important holidays were to her, I dragged myself to the nearby grocery store and bought a plant for a Mother's Day gift. I planned to stay with her for the next several days. At her kitchen table, after my mother served us both scrambled eggs and toast, which I managed to eat despite feeling sick, I presented the fern to her. I hoped she would be impressed.

But she didn't even say thank you. She went quiet and glowered at the plant.

I backed away slowly. Her eyes always looked shark-eye black when she was about to lose her temper. Before I could think of anything to say to distract her or redirect her anger, she chucked the apparently offensive gift at me. I dodged the plant. Its clay pot smashed against the wall and fell behind the stereo. I stared at the dirt smudge left behind, assessing the damage a moment too long. She rammed into me, knocking me into the stereo cabinet. Its glass edge dug into the upper right side of my rib cage.

She yelled and called me "ungrateful," and as her voice grew louder, I ran toward the stairs to my bedroom. But I couldn't get away fast enough. She threw me against the steps and pummeled me until I managed to break loose and scampered upstairs. My room was in a converted attic space with a tiny bathroom at one end and a sloping ceiling pitched so low that I risked bumping my head if I didn't walk exactly in the center. Inside the corner of the bathroom, I threw open the plywood panel to the crawl space where we kept extra toilet paper and storage boxes and dove inside.

In the dark, I heard her continue to yell after me, but eventually, her heavy footfalls returned downstairs. Though it was finally quiet, I knew it would take a long time for her to calm down. I spent what seemed like hours hiding in there, my body locked in a crouched position. The space was too small for her to reach me. This I knew, but I was still scared she might return. I imagined her knocking the walls down with a sledgehammer.

As I cowered, my adrenaline pumping wildly, I realized fear was worse than physical injury. Not ever knowing and relentlessly worrying about what mood she might be in or how enraged she might become, was in some ways a harsher punishment than the eventual melodramatic culmination of her temper. Fear was crouching in a crawl space and waiting to see how much more violence she would unleash. Fear prevented me from living, from making decisions. Fear kidnapped any sense of agency or control. It made me weak and passive. Since my focus was always on saying or doing whatever would cause the least amount of turmoil, I'd reduced myself to being a cheerleader, the most attentive listener, a people pleaser, avoiding my own interpretations and feelings, favoring everyone else's comfort over my own. I hated this about myself, but at the time I didn't understand that it was intertwined with survival.

In that crawl space waiting for the next, potentially fatal round, my fear did something unexpected. It hardened into anger. No one was going to rescue me or stop the abuse. People saw what they wanted to see. They were busy with their careers, daily routines, and other obligations. If I wanted anything to change, I would have to make it happen myself.

I decided that I was finished with my mother. My mother as she was that day.

When I was a young child, she used to acknowledge that she'd slipped and didn't mean to scare me or hurt me. This meant that she accepted responsibility and was capable of change. And the good moments kept me comfortably in denial, like how she hand-sewed my Halloween costumes and drove me to ballet classes.

She had struggled with a pattern of mental health issues for as long as I'd been alive. During psychotic episodes, she would hear God's voice telling her to end both of our lives. Once, the voice told her to wait on the railroad tracks until a train arrived to run us over; then a year later, she deliberately crashed our car on a rural highway. I'd learned how to placate her to steer us back onto slightly more stable ground, long enough to survive. And no matter how bizarre the episode, back then, she would return to reality at some point by getting back on medication, seeing her therapist, and apologizing. Since she deeply regretted her actions, I would always forgive her. She was more than her illness, and I believed she would find a way to change.

During check-ins with my mother's therapist after each major episode, I fixated on whether my mother could hear what I said over the classical waiting room music, and I probably didn't reveal as much as I should have. Still, I'll never forget how her therapist nonchalantly looked at me from across her desk and advised me to stay in my mother's home because if I didn't, if I decided to leave as my dad had, then my mother might kill herself. The heaviness of her statement haunted me.

What I finally considered for the first time on that violent Mother's Day was that even if leaving meant my mother would kill herself, I still had to go through with it. My life was in danger. The molten anger helped me realize that anything was better than another day in fear. It wasn't safe to continue living in denial. I couldn't continue letting fear suffocate me. I had to save my own life.

It was quiet on the other side of the plywood panel. The only sounds were my nervous breaths and pumping heart. I carefully crept out of the crawl space and onto the bathroom's linoleum floor. Since my mother and I had only recently moved into this house there were still many unpacked boxes scattered about. On the counter just outside of the small bathroom was a roll of garbage bags. I quickly filled two with the clothes I'd already put away inside my dresser drawers: jeans, T-shirts, and underwear. I hoisted the bags over my shoulders and walked back down the stairs.

My mother was waiting for me on the sofa.

"What do you think you're doing?" she asked.

"Leaving," I said, dropping one of the bags so I could open the front door.

She charged toward me. I tried to get out of the way, but I wasn't fast enough. She kicked me hard in the back, wearing the white Tretorn sneakers she wore most days. I toppled forward and fell off the front step, face down onto the grass, still damp with morning dew.

I gingerly pushed myself back up and watched her throw the garbage bags after me. My clothes flew across the lawn.

"Get out and don't ever come back! Selfish ingrate bitch!" she screamed.

But she didn't slam the door. She stood there, glaring, as I shoved my clothes as fast as I could back into the bags. I lugged everything to my dad's apartment almost two miles away, on the other side of Falls Church, Virginia, a suburb of Washington, DC.

Each time a car passed, I braced myself, expecting it to be my mother. Exhausted from mono and in pain from the beating, I stopped several times on the sidewalk to rest. When I finally arrived at my dad's apartment, no one answered. He wasn't expecting me, and I didn't yet have a key, so I nestled between the two garbage bags and slept on his front stoop until he returned that night.

My estrangement from my mother began that Mother's Day when I was fourteen, but it wasn't a clean break. The divorce dragged out over two years, and even though I was required to state for the record, in the judge's chambers, away from the courtroom audience and my mother's glare, that I wished to live full-time with my father, I still attempted to maintain a relationship with my mother. I visited her on weekends and holidays. I still loved her, and the warning of her therapist stayed with me.

But over time, as I became an adult, her behavior worsened. She made incessant, threatening phone calls and menacing unannounced visits. She called one of my employers and the president of the board of directors I served on and harassed them too. After I became more secretive about my contact information, she called the emergency line in the city where she heard from relatives I resided and fabricated stories about me overdosing and killing myself so the police would race to my apartment and pound on my door at all hours. I eventually got restraining orders and lived most of my adult life in hiding. Even her former therapist, the one who'd advised me to stay, had to relocate her office and home and enforce restraining orders against my mother.

My dad began his journey out of denial during his separation from my mother. He has apologized many times since then for leaving me with my mother and suggested I write about all that happened and even told me not to go easy on him.

While I'll probably continue processing this for the rest of my life, I forgave my dad because he acknowledged his mistake, deeply regretted it, and spent the rest of his lucid years doing more to be present in my life.

One of the best things he did was introduce me to the woman who became my stepmom. A petite blond with a sharp intellect and a devoted passion for the underdog, she works as a consumer advocate and embodies someone dedicating their talents and skills to try to make the world better. She brought me to some of my first protests, nurtured and supported my interest in theater and writing, took me to see Broadway plays, toured colleges with me and made sure I applied, taught me how to use the New York City subway system, and was one of the first family members to meet my daughter after her birth.

My stepmom entering my life when I was a devastated teen was like the sun finally coming out after a fourteen-year hurricane. My paternal grandmother always referred to her as "our guardian angel" because she made everything in our lives brighter.

No doubt my life would have turned out quite differently if it weren't for my stepmom.

She is the mother I never had.

But, as my daughter constantly points out, I do not call her "Mom." It isn't because I don't love her as though she is my mother. I do. It is because my associations to the name "Mom" and even to the role of motherhood have been severely altered by the past. I almost didn't become a mother for similar reasons.

To me, Mom is my biological mother, and for as long as we're both alive I will continue allowing the space for the possibility of change—but from a safe distance. It's highly probable we will never see each other again.

My feelings about my estrangement from my biological mother change frequently because they are entangled with my frustration over the lack of social resources for people in need. Our mental health system has largely been replaced with a prison system. But the shifting foundation of my feelings rests on my rock-solid belief that all people, no matter what mistakes or bad behavior they may have exhibited, no matter what mental health issues they may be grappling with, have the capacity to change, to do better. And allowing space for that possibility, which is not quite as emotionally demanding as forgiveness, is to treat others as well as ourselves with dignity.

I hope that my daughter will find it easier to draw the line between protecting herself and preserving the hope that someone might change for the better. I hope she will never be in a situation that requires her to make such a devastating but necessary decision.

Her persistent questions have helped me navigate motherhood and estrangement, and while we may not see our family reflected in mainstream narratives yet, what I hope my daughter will eventually glean from our story is the importance of saying no to abuse.

It took years for me to overcome the dread and phantom physical pain that Mother's Day brought on. While my daughter is still too young to learn the full story, I respond truthfully to her questions about my "other mommy" by pointing out that "Gaia," as she calls my stepmom, "is your grandmother, and we love her." This year, when we gathered for brunch, my stepmom surprised me with a beautiful calla lily, which I eagerly planted in my daughter's fairy garden outside our home, a refuge enshrouded by forest where we've lived her entire life. Providing stability for my child is proof that negative patterns can be broken, and growth is possible.

For me, Mother's Day will always be both sad and triumphant. Sad because my mother needed help and her illness caused her to behave in a cruel manner that has only led to being ensnared in the prison system and living unhoused. Triumphant because I finally prioritized my well-being instead of waiting for someone else to do so. I stood up for myself and changed my own life. It is my personal Independence Day.

Can't You Read?

Anna Qu

My aunt says she's like me—we're the same, fatherless children. Both our fathers passed away and our mothers remarried, bringing us into their new family. This assimilation has had repercussions, like that of separation and loss, from our mothers, their other children, and these children's fathers. Stories like ours are common in China. *Ming-ah*, she clicks her tongue, shaking her head as if she pities our fate, as if our fathers' deaths are our destiny.

I always thought it was strange that my family blamed misfortunes on fate but never on any culprit. My mother used to say it was too bad my father was dead, otherwise my life would be different—better. Her words felt cold and cruel, like she refused to take responsibility for me, but with my aunt, I'm learning it's a common cultural theme to blame fate instead of the government, society, or persons involved. As if my estrangement is a matter of fate instead of choice.

My mother is the person who holds the reins in my family, the one who told my half siblings it was their house and not mine; it was their father, not mine; it was my *ming*, not theirs.

After surviving generations of propaganda, I wondered if the collective trauma rooted in our history is inescapable within the family hierarchy. No one gets away unharmed. *We were born into a bitter life*, my aunt says as she pats me roughly on the back, as if the cards we're dealt in life are the only cards we can hold.

It's the summer of 2018 and my first time back in China since I left the country at the age of seven. It's hard to say why it's taken so long to return, but after my father's death, my mother's survival strategy was to keep moving forward. She never talked about my father or our past; her life was now with her new husband and their two growing children. I was a burden of that past, a scarlet reminder, a shame she couldn't quite shake. I often wondered why she brought me to America to live with her and her new family if she didn't want me there.

Twenty-seven years later, estranged from my immediate family, I arrive in Wenzhou in thick August humidity and meet my father's older sister. My aunt is in her seventies, shrunken and slightly hunched over but healthy and full of vigor. She wears a loose burgundy blouse with wide, loose slacks and simple canvas flats. I have no memories of her, but she tells me stories of when she babysat me as a toddler. *You loved to be chased and were always laughing.* Some things she says are easy to understand, while others feel muddled in nuances of our native Wenzhounese dialect. As long as it's conversational, I can keep up, but anything with depth seems just beyond my comprehension. I want to remain grateful for what I retain, instead of focusing on the increasing loss of words and language, another cost of assimilating.

As we finish up breakfast—fan tuans, a sticky rice ball stuffed with pickled vegetables, shredded pork, and fried dough—she rattles off the buses we must take to get to my grandfather's grave. *Do you want to pick something up?* she asks with an expectant smile. *You can't go empty-handed.* I'm not sure what one brings to respect the dead, but I nod in agreement. I'm grateful for her generosity, taking me to see my maternal grandfather after all she has suffered growing up in my father's family. I wonder if she goes out of her way *because* she's had the life she did. Before I can finish my thought or drain the last of my hot soy milk, she's rushing us out of the hotel lobby.

When I started planning this trip to China, I didn't know my aunt existed. No one in my family had ever spoken about her, not my grandmother, my mother, my aunts, or my twenty or so cousins. Her existence, like mine, is taboo, invisible after the death of her father. Her station in the family would be forever altered—expected to serve the family, recognized as servant instead of daughter or sibling. It was the same expectation waiting for me in America after I arrived to join my mother's new family, only I had no idea. Our fathers' deaths marked the beginning of our hardships, not the end. With our mothers remarried, we lost more than just our fathers; we lost our entire family.

Perhaps the familiarity I feel with my aunt comes from the silence we've been forced to occupy our entire lives. I ask her if she talks to any of her half siblings now. She looks at me and shakes her head sadly. *Not for many years*, she whispers. She tells me they never treated her like a sister, just the family help. Tears stream down her face as she recalls the way they bullied her, calling her dumb and useless. How they once framed her for stealing, how they ran her out of the house eventually. *Why,*

why did they do that? she asks me. I pat her arm and tell her not to cry. I don't have any answers for her. *Don't say any more,* I find myself responding, even though I've come for these stories. There's an ache in my chest as I think of my half siblings. They are lost to me too. I blink dust out of my eyes and swallow the dry lump in my throat.

We walk in silence, and I take in the world around us. The streets of my hometown are wide, newly paved, and busy with traffic. My aunt walks briskly, opening a black umbrella over us as soon as our strides match. I'm tall and awkward next to her shrinking body. I take in the architecture and landscape, the sounds and smells. Wenzhou has been an industrial city since the 1980s, but the poverty of the sixties and seventies is still evident today in suburban neighborhoods, abandoned and left in ruins. The labor force began in small-scale production, products like badges, labels, shoes, plastic bags, various trinkets, and later shifted to large-scale leather, purses, and toy factories. Given the economic developments since then, the rich live in new high-rises and the poor live in slums and half-demolished buildings out of sight. Modernity has brought major class divide. *New developments,* she points proudly, *all skyscrapers.* Two obtuse glass buildings sticking out of the town landscape. A lot has changed in twenty-seven years, but I'm relieved the land feels familiar under my feet.

We arrive at a paved lot with half a dozen minibuses with various destinations flashing in bright neon orange across the display. I can pick out a word or two but can't decipher meaning or destination from the simplified Chinese. *Which bus are we taking?*

Can you read the signs? she asks me. Our eyes meet. Embarrassingly, I can't. I wipe the shame from my face as if wiping away dirt and sweat.

Lin, what's this word? my mother asked my stepfather years ago while he was reading his Taiwanese newspaper, a nightly ritual of his. My stepfather turned his gaze to my mother's perfectly manicured finger and read the character to her. I don't recall the word, but my half brother, still in elementary school, happened to be in the dining room with us and asked what I didn't dare to: *Why doesn't mom know that word?* We were all silent for a moment, waiting. *Because mom didn't grow up as lucky as you,* my stepfather responded. *She didn't have much schooling, not like you will.*

This was news to me. I wonder now if my mother keeps moving forward because backward are the remains of too many emotions, all of which amount to her helplessness. Decades after that conversation, I asked my grandmother if any of her children went to high school. She paused to crack a sunflower seed between her teeth. *Your youngest uncle went for a year but never finished. They all had to work.*

Can you read? An explanation is lodged in my throat: I've studied Chinese at various stages of my life but couldn't retain much while living in New York. After college, I spent a year in Taiwan, teaching English and studying Chinese, but as soon as I returned, the knowledge evaporated like dew in midday sun, leaving only water stains. I think of my grandmother, only a few years my aunt's senior. She only spoke our provincial dialect, Wenzhounese, and couldn't read and write. Like many of her generation, she married young and never went to school.

What about you? Can you read? I ask my aunt gently, careful not to wound her. She looks at me as if she's holding on to a secret under her tongue and gives me a look that says she's gotten away with something she shouldn't have. *A little bit.* I smile at her small rebellion. We stand side by side and try to make out the destination on a bus together for a time. Between the two of us, one old, one relatively young, we equal one literate person.

Pedestrians pass around us, climbing into packed buses. My aunt directs us onto an old, dusty minibus with no air conditioning. A woman in her late forties is crouched on a plastic stool near the entrance of the bus, a busted tin money box on her lap. She's collecting coins and giving out ticket stubs.

How much to the end of the line? my aunt asks in Wenzhounese. I look up at the indecipherable writing in front of the bus and realize that, unlike NYC public transportation, the fares vary depending on where you get on and off.

She nods her head at the sign. *It's written right there. Can't you read?* The ticket agent clearly understands Wenzhounese and yet responds in Mandarin. The commotion on the bus hushes as eyes turn.

I'm sorry, little sister, my aunt apologizes, bowing her head and exposing her neck. *I don't recognize words.*

What a nuisance! the woman complains, loud enough for everyone to hear. My aunt looks down sheepishly, acquiescing, *Thank you, thank you.* A knot rises to my throat as I watch the interaction, wanting to defend my aunt but unable to find words, the language, the means. Her humiliation is my humiliation. The agent rolls her eyes, and I find I am mute, seething with anger at the way my aunt is being treated.

Why was she so mean to you? I ask as soon as my aunt slides into the seat next to me.

It's nothing, just my ming.

Why is it fate when someone is an asshole to you, I want to

shout. Why didn't she stand up for herself? Why did she accept the way people treated her instead of demanding equality and respect? The air on the bus is still and suffocating as we wait for the bus to move. I think about the type of life my aunt must tolerate, a world where she is a second-class citizen because she is fatherless, uneducated, and a woman. She is at the mercy of her community.

I slide the window open and stick my nose out. Literacy in the region has historically been low. Education is not a requirement for the cheap workforce, especially for people like my grandmother and aunt and my extended family. It was never made a priority, yet the uneducated are looked down upon and treated biasedly. I see the divide as clearly as the rift that caused estrangement in our family, and it's hard for me to look away. My aunt is dependent on the decency of the people around her to get her to where she needs to go. To be able to stand up for yourself is a privilege, one that most people cannot assume or demand, and the rage leaves a bloated heaviness in my limbs. I bristle at her explanation and the generations of mistreatment we must tolerate here. It's an inadequacy that my body knows how to store.

Back in the States, I carefully built myself around education and opportunity, a writer who uses words to be heard and to defend. I am able-bodied, educated, successful. But here, I am partially illiterate, mute, and invisible, forced once again into the role of a child, under an authority that shaped society in a way I do not condone but in which I was compelled to exist. To be here is to be aware of the seven generations before my own, and the legacy of hardship on this relentless, arid land. To be here is to be powerless again, to feel the complicated encumbrance of culture and womanhood. I feel shattered, and the shattering is that of safety, protection, and autonomy. Perhaps this is why my mother refuses to return. Perhaps this is why I need to return to this reality, to feel the past so that I can bear the present. To be closer to my origin story. To understand how I began. The yearning for family, for my mother, for love and fairness, started here.

I wonder if estrangement is inevitable for people like my aunt and me, just like the way the uneducated are treated. That, I am coming to realize, is why I am here. I am looking for an answer: Is it my fault I'm estranged from my family? Or is it cultural? Is it just the ordinary cruelty of power dynamics in a communist country? I blamed my mother for my estrangement, for the way she divided my siblings and me. We are all her kids; why couldn't she treat us equally? I blame her just the way I blame the bus attendant. I want my aunt to do the same, to stand up against those who treat her unfairly, but to what end? What about the next person who mistreats her? In America, I didn't need to fight the world; my only conflict was with my mother. The irony is she was the person I cared about the most, the one I sought to teach me right from wrong.

I swallow another lump in my throat. I haven't seen my mother in a decade, and the passage of time is a constant reminder of the gaping wound between us. I worry that I am allowing too much time to pass. I worry she will grow old and feeble and die before we reconcile. But I also know from experience that this yearning, this dull pain of want, is more tolerable than the pain we cause each other.

We get off the minibus at the end of the line and scramble into a second waiting minibus. The same conversation ensues; my aunt waits patiently and asks the ticket agent for cost and directions. She can't read, so she needs to use what she has: her desperation and her willingness to submit. She uses her warm, disarming smile. This ticket agent, exhausted and possibly close to a heatstroke, does not respond and slips her two stubs and change. There will be no abuse from this agent, and I relax.

The bus takes us to the outskirts of the city, into a thick smog of soot left by other traffic. Out in the country, there are fewer cars, and older motorized vehicles, scooters, and bikes fill the road. It's well past noon by the time we take a rickshaw to the base of a mountain. The bus rides plastered our skin in sweat that the rickshaw cakes up in new layers of smoke and grime. We pass what feels like miles of rubble, construction workers with shirts wrapped around their heads, a wet ring watermarking their shoulders. Their bodies are leathery from the sun, their hands white from carrying rocks and broken-down cement. When we come to a stop, I'm grateful for the umbrella my aunt pulls out, giving us shade as we climb the thousand feet up a worn unmarked path and overgrown foliage.

Does this mountain have a name? I ask, wondering how I'll ever find it again.

No. She shrugs. *Most of these small mountains are nameless.* I find her response perplexing. How many places remain nameless nowadays? At the same time, I'm strangely comforted by the lack of need to name, to identify or process. The irony of traveling seven thousand miles to hike a nameless mountain is not lost on me. Before I can respond, we reach a narrow clearing and a wide blue sky.

It's a quiet spot. My grandfather's tomb is made of cool gray slate, grand as a coliseum, with a thatched gazebo and three steps leading up to a tall headstone etched in carved calligraphy.

It feels fitting; he was a stoic man of few words. When he married my mother off, his youngest daughter, he nodded and said, *One less mouth to feed.* It was a resentment my mother replayed over and over in my childhood. Still, he and my grandmother took me in when my father passed and my mother went to pursue her American dream. I remember chopstick fights with him over the last piece of beef tongue, gizzard, and pork belly. I recall the murky smell of his pipe, and his stubbornness over giving up the habit that would claim his life.

It's taken me twenty-seven years and most of the morning to get here: a nameless mountain with an expansive view of an unimpressive, nondescript smoggy skyline. Off to either side are a few other graves, quietly growing weed and collecting debris. We pause to mop the sweat off our brows and neck and swat at bugs.

The feng shui is very good here, my aunt comments, taking in the mood, before adding, *Let's tidy the grave.*

Using our hands, we pluck the weed growing between the cracks of the slate. We pick with our fingers, dig with our nails. We remove the old flowers, dried and half blown away, and scrap what debris we can with our bare palms, the skin of our fingers as rags. The stone works as a dull knife on our knuckles and tender fingertips. My aunt pulls weeds efficiently and hastily, with no concern for her hands, and I try my hardest to do the same without wincing in pain, without protecting myself. She's better at it than me.

We don't have incense to light, so we stand straight, press our hands together, bow at the waist three times, and pay our respects. *Azi, I'm here,* I say without knowing exactly what I mean. *I've made it back. I'm here.*

At times, it feels like the weight of our history is what makes *ming* inescapable. But what about the choices we make? Don't they mean anything? I wonder about the efforts we take, like the step I've taken to return to China, the cycle of abuse I've overcome, the book I've written, the path of healing I continue to chart for myself. There is no response to my questions, only a calming breeze rustling the tops of trees, the hardness of the granite headstone flickering in the light, what remains of my grandfather carried by the wind. *Ming* knows where we've been but not where we are going, how we'll get there, or what we'll achieve. However circuitous, my aunt and I are shattering preconceived notions set for us. Maybe even if we remain nameless like this mountain we stand on, it can be enough to have been here and to know this truth.

We lay out the oranges and wilting flowers as an offering. I snap a photo of the calligraphy I cannot read, a grandfather I barely remember, values set in calcified stone still alive in his descendants.

Afterward, as we trek down the nameless mountain, my aunt breaks the silence and says we can get a cab back to the hotel. Confused, I asked her why we didn't take a cab directly to the gravesite instead of two buses and a rickshaw. She gives me an embarrassed look and says simply, *This is the only way I know how to get here.*

I don't know how to respond. I'm struck again by the limitation illiteracy breeds, the effect it has on navigating daily life. It's an ingrained burden no one wants to see or hear and yet is very much alive in older generations. I glance around, looking for landmarks and geographical indicators of where we are. How do you remember a place if you can't read or write and can't mark the site? How can you fully participate in any system, society, or culture? You can only chart the road that is already paved for you, over and over. There are no signs, in English or Chinese, or perspective at the bottom of the mountain. I sense that I don't have a better solution and all I can do is accept what she's telling me and commit to memory the path she's taught me.

As we wait for the cab, I think about the connection between illiteracy and the limited relationship I have with my family. Both are a type of severing, one to access and the other, to my roots. Illiteracy is alienation from language, a rupture in independence and community, our deserved place in our larger society. It's akin to my separation from family and the unfairness I felt. A rupture that is not mine alone to hold, I am realizing. We, the estranged, are those who cannot abide by the rules of the greater family unit or society.

In visiting this familiar land, the place that I once called home, maybe I can forge a connection that heals instead of wounds. Perhaps this journey is about finding a new pathway toward belonging and ancestry, as if excavating an old, familiar language. I can continue to sow new roots, and it'll be up to me to decide where they will lead.

A Leap of Logic

Emi Nietfeld

I love a hot take. Nothing makes me feel alive like trash-talking the latest op-eds while shredding straw wrappers. In dim Manhattan bars, my long hair falls over the table as I summarize faulty reasoning to my friends, offering, "Isn't that preposterous?"

Recently, I reviewed a memoir by a conservative internet personality about how family—nuclear family—is the most important thing; no job or education will ever fill the gaping void of our defective caregivers. I read it with an open mind: Like the author, I spent time in foster care; like him, I don't speak to my parents; our tumultuous childhoods taught us not to take stability, love, or respect for granted. But as the book went on, its claims became more and more absurd and contradictory before devolving into harmful tropes.

As I dissect the tangled reasoning, energy pulses through my body. I am most myself, even as I'm shocked by my conviction. Just a few years ago, this exercise would've filled me with shame, certain that I was missing something. I struggled to form opinions. All my college essays came back scrawled: "Needs a thesis." But who was I to make an argument? I was always so aware that someone—my mom—could, and likely would, point out that I was wrong. She would speak in circles until I was dizzy, always holding the trump card: *I made you.*

My problem transcended English class: I couldn't grasp logic. Until I was twenty-six, I couldn't write proofs, follow deductive reasoning, or even finish sudoku puzzles. Whenever I was confronted with implications I was supposed to put together, my mind went white. A deafening static filled my ears. How could other people be so confident that X and Y meant Z? Didn't they have someone whispering over their shoulder, urging them to always doubt themselves and defer to the person who knew better?

In college, I suffered through a computer science major despite these handicaps because I craved something unassailable that no one could argue with. The code would work or it wouldn't, and for once, my mom's opinion didn't matter.

I learned to suspend my disbelief early. At Baptist school, I was told that the earth was ten thousand years old. Evolutionists had forged all the fossils. There was one unassailable truth, and it was the Bible. When the Good Book contradicted itself, it was still true: Every fact in the world could be contorted to fit.

We listened to the radio constantly so we'd never forget. My mom sang along to Faith 900 KTIS in her Oldsmobile; Dr. James Dobson's Focus on the Family punctuated my parents' pointed silence in our Minnesota duplex; the classical station that played only Christian composers accompanied my father's minivan lectures.

The lesson didn't just apply to the Lord's word but to every element of life. To simply assume the most obvious conclusion was to act without faith, to be a bad Christian, a bad person, a bad daughter.

My mom was a once-beautiful woman, like an actress made up to look normal: harried, with graying eyebrows, a billfold bulging from her slacks. Despite her difficult daughter and the baggage of a brutal divorce, she somehow still shone with optimism. She was the type of person you wanted to believe.

"I think my daughter has ADD," she told the psychologist when I was eleven. She glowed in her role as "responsible parent." She'd brought me in at the first sign of trouble, right after she'd won custody and my father moved 1,200 miles away. My mom detailed my symptoms: I was disorganized, disheveled, and chronically late.

Sitting on the sofa next to her, I fumed. How could this man with a PhD believe that the problem was all me? "Come to the house!" I begged him, trying to explain that my mom was a hoarder, a word I didn't know at the time. We owned at least five alarm clocks, but they were buried in heaps of detritus my mom called "the abyss"; our only shower overflowed with empty Aquafina bottles she forbade me to throw away. My mom got to work late every day, greasy-haired, often missing her badge. Even as a tween, I was old enough to question: What did it mean for an eleven-year-old to be "disorganized"? How could a child be "chronically late"?

But no one really challenged my mom, so I figured she must have had a point. The evaluation consisted of three questionnaires. At our second appointment, the psychologist referred us to the psychiatrist who wrote me a prescription for ADHD medication.

My mom had a knack for creating her own world. She forged it out of nothing. It was one of my favorite things about her. Our life felt objectively shitty: We lived in a freezing apartment where mice scuttled around piles of old art supplies. We never had enough money after credit card statements and lawyers' bills. My mom, a crime scene photographer, spent her days in a windowless lab that stank of chemicals, printing out photos of dead people and filing them into envelopes.

And yet, what two people ever lived more of a charmed life? We ate at Baja Del Sol, splitting a burrito made cheaper by a grocery store receipt, eating enormous quantities of free chips and salsa. We pretended we starred in a reality TV show.

"I almost got into Stanford," my mom said to anyone who would listen, pushing her glasses up on her nose. "They only rejected me because I was sixteen."

Could she ever really know why she didn't get in, I wondered as a child. But with the way she said it, she made the California palm trees wave. I could almost feel the kiss of the sun on my face, my hair bleached, my cheeks freckled in that other life that just barely elided her.

And in that creation, it was almost my life too. Her dreams, in a way, became my fate. To the doctors and physician's assistants who gave me Ritalin, then Adderall, and eventually antipsychotics, I was "a middling student," of average intelligence "at best." But to my mom, I was a brilliant genius, destined for the incredible success she'd been denied.

The only problem was when someone disagreed with my mom.

She was a loyal friend who memorized the shifts of her favorite cashiers. She always had her eye out for what gadget a coworker might want and for sales on a neighbor's favorite candies. Whenever she heard sirens, she prayed for the people in the ambulance.

Almost as passionate was her list of enemies. Nothing could temper the venom toward my father, her father, my half brother's father. Anyone who'd wronged her. By the time I was eleven, the list included me.

The conflict started with my parents' divorce. My parents had wed six weeks after meeting; ten years in, they hated each other. My mom was the breadwinner and did all the housework yet insisted that husbands had to lead the family. My father, in turn, could be cruel to both of us: criticizing my mom's homemaking, lambasting her for wearing pants, spanking me for crying out of hunger, waging an overarching vendetta against fun. As a child, I understood my father's flaws and forgave, but my mother could not tolerate the disrespect. I considered this a defect of her character. Meanwhile, I saw how my mom pushed my dad's buttons: She was always right, lied when it suited her, and wouldn't hesitate to brandish a bygone wound to win an argument.

When I was nine, my parents separated. I was so relieved.

But during the custody battle, my mom took me to the therapist and announced, "I'm gathering evidence." She wanted me to provide a full-throated confession of my father's abuse: physical, emotional, and sexual. I'm sure she believed it was true. In elementary school, I'd gotten frequent yeast infections, which hadn't been bad enough to intervene in the moment, but looking back became, to my mom, a smoking gun. Besides, she had a feeling. Worst of all, I loved my father more—the most damning evidence of grooming and exploitation.

The therapist prodded, but I had nothing to say. I resented the corporal punishment I'd received, but both my parents agreed with "spare the rod, spoil the child." My family had strange boundaries, but my father's were no worse than my mom's.

I was aware of how desperately my mom wanted to be my savior, how she wanted us to be hurt—and heal—together. She inventoried the damage wrought by her ex-husband and assumed that I must have been equally scarred.

But when I refused to tell the story she wanted, little by little, she turned on me. She had spent years and tens of thousands of dollars fighting my father for sole custody, and I wasn't even grateful.

"Why did you even get married?" I screamed at her. "You knew it was a horrible idea! My dad didn't even want kids!"

Before she had me, my mom had dreamed of a second child, a blond daughter to call Honey. My half brother had begged her not to get remarried, a story she told while laughing. My father had not wanted to be a parent, had threatened to move out when my mom got pregnant, a story she told snickering. She had me at forty; I was her last chance. All that was supposed to make me more thankful, not less. *I went to all this work to have you*, she told me. *I am the one who conjured you into being.*

My mom believed in repressed memories: Just because I couldn't remember my father abusing me didn't mean it hadn't happened.

She kept trying to take me to Theophostic Prayer, where a counselor would lay hands on me and pray for Jesus to flash back the events that led to my tween anger. My mom dragged me to an exorcist who screamed that she could see Satan in my eyes. My mom offered me *The Courage to Heal*, which communicated the message: If you believe you've been abused and your life shows the symptoms, then you probably were. Just like church, all it took was "belief": a conscious choice to remind myself every minute of every day of what I wanted to be true and will it to be such. But this time, I refused.

I'd been raised on parables of men blasted in Nebuchadnezzar's furnace, of Daniel stranded in the lion's den, Queen Esther risking her death for a chance to save her people. Just a few years earlier, I'd knelt beside my bed and prayed to die a martyr. But whatever sense of self I had wouldn't let me give into my mother. Besides, I simply wasn't a good enough liar.

If I could have cut ties with my mom right then, I would have. After all, I'd begged the custody evaluators to let me live with my dad. I didn't think that would be perfect, but I'd sensed it would be better. Instead, the judge ruled we could only speak through mediation—I never saw my father again.

I was stuck with my mom. She hauled me to psychiatrists and punitive therapy, desperately trying to save me. As an Evangelical, it was her obligation to convert me, to drag me to her side no matter how much I fought or resisted, no matter the cost.

The professionals seemed to agree that I was the problem. I was prescribed a dozen psychotropic medications in two years. At fourteen, I was locked in an institution for nine months, to learn to take responsibility for my bad attitude and conflicts with my mom.

"Focus on what you can control," the counselors scolded me. But I couldn't control my mom. Our relationship was a given: no one suggested distancing myself, even when I went to foster care my sophomore year of high school and when her hoarding meant I slept in my car at sixteen. Even when my mom couldn't take care of me physically, the tie was psychic and irrevocable: She'd willed me into existence; how could I survive without her?

With each passing year, I took it for granted that my mom was all I had, my only ally, the parent who signed forms and helped me go to summer camp. By the end of high school, I accepted that there was no escape hatch, no other world than the one where I contorted my reality to fit hers.

Still, I did everything I could to separate myself. I applied to distant universities; I penned letters that felt like betrayals begging for scholarships; I prepared to not ask anything of my mom, not even a place to stay during breaks. Within a week of graduating from high school, I fled as far as I could imagine, backpacking on my own through Europe's cheapest cities.

One night in Budapest, two men working at a hostel set me up; one of them raped me. The next night, my passport missing, I came back frantically looking for it. My rapist was waiting for me. I remember nothing after that. I woke up in a different hostel with no memory of how I'd gotten there. Among my belongings was a photograph of the man laughing, taken during my blackout.

I was abroad for the first time, seventeen, alone, and broke—and worried I was injured. I tried calling my mom from pay phone after pay phone, desperate for her comfort and absolution, hopeful she could explain what had happened and give me a path forward.

Instead, her advice complicated the brutal facts. It didn't matter that two men had trapped me, that the accomplice was likely standing guard just outside the door. It was irrelevant that my rapist yelled at me and called me a bitch, held me so I couldn't move and couldn't breathe. It meant nothing that he attacked me again the next day.

What mattered was the single beer I'd had earlier that night. My mom chided me for "trusting" the hostel's employees enough to chitchat with them in the kitchen. The problem, my mom informed me, was that I hadn't objected forcefully enough. She emailed: "Next time make up your mind to say 'no' and walk away, loudly and clearly."

For the next eight years, I lay awake at night reconstructing the assault, contorting the details into a scenario where I'd simply been too naive to express my preferences and my rapist wasn't a rapist at all, just a middle-aged man giving me exactly what I'd asked for. Anything was easier than challenging my mom's version of events. I was filled with shame; she was nothing but conviction.

It seemed like I could rewrite my memories with enough effort, but then some image I'd managed to forget poked through—my rapist laughing at me while I cried, the other man walking back in at the end, the semen on my cardigan—shattering the whole illusion.

When I was twenty-six, I finally sought out trauma therapy. I didn't want to talk about my childhood or the divorce. Instead

I sensed that the assault, and my mom's response to it, exemplified the way she maintained a stranglehold on truth, one that she wielded to maintain power over me, even into my adulthood. I didn't want some nice lady to reassure me with platitudes about it not being my fault; her opinion would never outweigh my mom's. What I needed was an objective perspective.

I signed up for exposure therapy, a methodical cognitive-behavioral treatment. Hyperventilating and crying, I told the story again and again, describing every taste, smell, sound, and sensation. Then my counselor and I examined these details as evidence, trying to understand the truth.

After the first exposure session, my therapist folded his hands and broke the news: "It sounds like you were attacked." I stopped breathing and clutched the edge of my chair. Somewhere, a building was collapsing, everyone inside of it dying in the rubble. The situation seemed obvious to my therapist. He flipped through his notes. "He nearly choked you to death," he said, "several times." Everything pointed to the assault being planned, the act of someone practiced. At the end of our session, my therapist posed the question, "Why do you think the other man came back in at the end?"

I could not connect the dots. All I could think about was my mom. How could it be planned if she didn't say so? How could things be as straightforward as this therapist thought? Years later, I would remark at the cliché of it all: I was raped by a forty-something-year-old stranger, maybe two. Trapped in a hostel where I was, suspiciously, the only guest.

But back then, all I could do was loop over my therapist's comments, as though his confidence could overwrite my mom's. Every day for homework, I had to replay recordings of our sessions. While hearing myself describe the horrors I'd denied made me writhe on the floor, clutching my Moroccan carpet, my therapist's voice was a balm and a beacon. It guided me through the darkness of my closed-eye recountings. The parts where he shared his interpretation, where he posed the hard questions that I still couldn't answer—those, I listened to again and again.

This whole time, I had been ready to forgive my mom. I had longed to be the bigger person. She lived in a house that reeked of urine, swerving in and out of crushing debt. Meanwhile I grew up and did the things she once dreamed of. I went to Harvard and moved to California to work in tech. I hung out under palm trees and parlayed my computer science degree into a lucrative career at Google. Perhaps I had an especially bad case of impostor syndrome, given that deduction still stumped me, but if anything, that made me work harder. Not unlike my mom's fantasy of landing an egalitarian medical student, I fell in love with a fellow software engineer and got married. Where my mom's life had been cursed, mine became charmed.

Her belief in me, as irrational as it was, had spurred me on. How else could I explain why I believed in myself? But while her faith in me fueled me, my faith in her tore me apart.

For years, I avoided asking her about the past, fearing what she'd say. When I finally did, she told me I'd been troubled as a teen. The night I was raped, I'd been drinking. Yes, they'd offered me a drink, I told her, but I remembered, clearly, refusing them. "You took the drink," she argued. "You took shots with them."

She was so convinced that eventually I convinced myself again. Could I have taken a drink? A shot? Sure, I decided. Anything to keep the peace.

In therapy, I resisted the truth, no matter how many Socratic questions my counselor asked me. No matter how hard I fought to evaluate the evidence, draw a conclusion, and stick to it—my bond with my mom still held, stronger than logic. It was where my umbilical cord attached to her placenta, my mouth to her breast, my first home.

It seemed like the only solution was to become mentally tough. I had to create a model of the world where both my mom and I could be right. But as each month passed, my nagging suspicion grew stronger: What if that was literally—logically—impossible?

Once I started therapy, I began ignoring my mom's texts. Each ping on my phone felt like an act of aggression. Sure, she was just asking if I wanted her to mail me one hundred tea candles or seventeen sticks of Mitchum deodorant, but it was also a reminder of how badly she could wound me. Every interaction veiled a threat that she could call me crazy, claim I had wanted it. She'd always have the upper hand.

I was always willing to reconsider my assumptions if a new fact emerged, to take responsibility. Truth, to me, was fragile: emerging from fallible memory, open to challenge, sacred. But her truth was a battering ram, ready to smash through any evidence. The conflict felt intractable. Even as I made progress in therapy, sometimes it seemed like the only solution was to kill myself.

I believed, from so many movies and stories about dysfunctional families that I could, and should, make things right. I was trying my hardest to heal us—even as I worried that it would cost me my life. But even that wasn't enough. I could die, and my mom would still be telling stories about the ungrateful daughter who sabotaged the custody battle, had a broken brain, and offered her body to perverted, dirty men.

I'd taken for granted that the only happy ending involved reconciliation, but when I started opening up to friends about my past, they asked me, "Do you still talk to your mom?" They seemed shocked when I replied, "Of course." I was stunned that estrangement was even an option—let alone one that outsiders found inevitable.

But I didn't want to go no contact. I just wanted the best parts of my mom. I wanted her forgiveness—although, for what, I couldn't pinpoint. I needed her to let me off the hook. If I just kept faith, I believed she'd change. The foggy windshield of my mind would clear. I'd become the daughter she adored and praised, even as she rose to the highest ideal I held for her. I'd fly her to Europe and we'd enjoy the Louvre and the Tate. One day, I'd introduce her to her grandchild without worrying one bit that she'd trash-talk me to my newborn.

The idea that I had a choice—that I *could* cut ties—made me squirm. But what if there was no way I could live with what happened to me, as long as every missed call from my mom made me feel like flames engulfed my limbs? What if there was such a thing as cause and effect, a simple logical leap staring me in the face?

Just before my twenty-seventh birthday, I called my mom again to ask for her version of events. I'd been writing and rewriting a book about my adolescence. Finally, I was finding clarity by talking to people from my past, comparing their recollections to my own and cross-referencing against an archive of records I'd compiled from hospitals, social workers, and therapists. But my mom's interviews bridged nothing; they only highlighted the gap. With each call, she seemed more adamant: I was the sick one, broken by my father; her hoarding was a quirk, not a problem; I had bad judgment with alcohol and men.

Listening to her describe this foolish, crazy daughter, someone so distant from me, I sensed then that if I cut the cord, I would feel better. I suspected that maybe my real life would begin. But I didn't want to make the call. I couldn't bear to say the words. My husband and I were traveling for a wedding the evening I worked up the courage. I called my mom, tears running down my face. "I can't talk to you anymore," I told her. "Not while you treat me like this."

She didn't understand, and I tried to explain. "You have to stop blaming me," I told her, listing out the aftermath of the divorce, my time in foster care, my assault.

She sighed, sounding annoyed. "What can I say to make you think I don't think it's your fault?"

"You can say, 'It's not your fault.'"

She stayed silent.

"I love you. I love you. I love you," I replied, as if I'd never say it again.

I was prepared for a chasm of grief to open in my chest. But I felt nothing but relief when I hung up the phone. My husband and I went to find dinner, then I slept late in our plush hotel bed. By the next morning, it no longer mattered what my mom thought: I wouldn't hear about it. The opinions that had hamstrung me for years, because our relationship relied on me accepting them, reduced into awful, ancient anecdotes that had no bearing on my choices.

Even though I told my mother not to get in touch, she wouldn't believe it. She kept texting me like nothing had happened. I had to block her number and her email address.

I wrote my story in cafés, shaking loose the doubt that shadowed my words. I poured over a cache of my old journals, desperate to make sure I recounted things correctly, and learned that I actually have an excellent memory.

Year by year, my voice has gotten bolder, especially as I've seen that my mom will use hers. She wrote a letter to the editor of a literary journal disputing an essay I published about my rape—a missive that, ironically, confirmed exactly what I'd written. She's told relatives that I'm mentally unstable; some seem to believe her. I find solace in seeing my worst fears come to pass and realizing that nothing bad happens.

Despite the agony of deciding to say goodbye, after four years without my mom's voice echoing in my head, I can't fathom living any other way. I can't imagine going back to cowering, unable to even finish a crossword puzzle. For years, I lived in terror. Now, I simply live. I read bad books and rage against them. I make new friends and, sometimes, enemies. It's okay if people don't like me. It's okay to be wrong.

Sometimes people on the internet tell me that I need to forgive and forget. I only have one mother, they say; life is short; stop being selfish. But letting go isn't always painful. While I'm grateful for the good things my mom did for me, I'm even more grateful to exist outside of her orbit. Going no contact has forced me to own my perspective. It's made me realize the power I have over who I allow into my life and how those people make me feel. In creating distance, I've found peace. Estrangement is a quiet space where I can think.

A Legacy of Estrangement

Lindsey Danis

Growing up, I knew my family was different from my friends' families and those I saw on television. I was an only child, my parents were divorced, and there were living relatives I did not know, because we did not speak to them.

Although I was too young to know the word "estrangement," I understood at a core level that something forbidden and shameful was taking place. Families fought—and my mostly Irish American extended clan were no exception—but at the end of the day, you made peace.

What terrible, awful thing had happened in my ancestry for there to be no peace? Why did it keep happening?

It was only later, when I stopped speaking to my father, that I realized I'd mined the old stories in search of a permission slip only I could give myself.

I was six when my parents separated. My mother realized she didn't love my father, had maybe never loved him. She'd done what had been expected of women at the time, perhaps even seeing marriage as an escape route from her own parents' drama. Post-divorce, my mother had several serious boyfriends, though she has not remarried.

My father remarried about a year after the divorce was finalized, though he remained angry at my mother—and by extension, at me. The thirty-minute car rides to his house were filled with grievances about court-ordered child support or prying questions about my mother's dating life. Shame turned my cheeks bright pink. I fell silent, NPR's *Marketplace* playing in the background. By the time he finished venting and asked about my day at school, my stomach was in knots and I'd prepared one-word answers that would get him off my back.

Mandated by the custody agreement to spend half the week with an authoritarian who could not see me through his resentment, I soon learned silence was my only weapon. Sitting and waiting for him to pick me up from my mother's, I would turn to stone. *You're going into your shell*, my mother would observe.

I thought of a snail, tender parts spiraled and tucked inside. I thought of crabs' soft bellies and fighting claws. I didn't want to fight or be on the defensive. All I wanted was to be left alone.

When my mother took my side, I was grateful. When she counseled me to keep trying to improve my relationship with my father, part of me began to wonder whether she was giving me the advice she had needed to hear.

My grandmother Chessie is rarely mentioned in my mother's childhood stories. When she is, my mother recalls regular bridge games with the neighbors. Booze flowed freely at the card table, day drinking hinting at the tedium and monotony of fifties-era housewifery. On bridge nights, Chessie made salad, a little luxury my mother adored.

Chessie was a girl from Covington, Kentucky, who wanted to see the world. When she met my grandfather, Steven, at an Army dance, at age eighteen, she saw her chance.

But Chessie's parents thought she was too young to be a bride. They gave her an ultimatum—them or him—and she chose him, moving north and getting married. When Chessie found herself alone in a new city, the luster of adventure wore off. She tried to return home while Steven was stationed in the Philippines during World War II, but her parents wanted nothing to do with her.

After my grandfather returned from service, they started a family. Chessie described her happiness at becoming a parent in her pregnancy journal: Once she had my mother to keep her company, she would no longer be lonely.

When I was a kid, the custody schedule dictated my every move. Growing older, I found creative ways to get around court mandates and avoid my father. Research projects, set painting for the school play—whatever plausible academic excuse would buy my freedom for a night. While I got what I wanted, my father held my little rebellion against me, using sighs and lectures to let me know I was a constant disappointment.

After I left for college, I spent only one night at his house. "This means so much to me," my father said, laying a camping mat in the living room on Christmas Eve because they'd converted my old bedroom to a formal dining room. *I don't care*, I thought. If he actually cared, he wouldn't serve brisket for Christmas dinner, knowing I hadn't eaten red meat since middle school. He wouldn't gripe about child support payments or college tuition, painful reminders that my worth as a person was not inherent but conditional.

My mother's parents divorced when she was in college. Chessie pestered my mother for information about my grandfather's new girlfriends and where he was living. My mother was busy dating my father and going to beach parties with her sorority sisters. She resented her mother's questions and being asked to choose sides. Eventually, there was a breakdown in her relationship with Chessie, and they stopped speaking.

Even as I tried to fit into my father's new family, talking about books with my stepmother or playing in the backyard with my two much-younger half brothers, I knew I could do what my mother had done. I could cut him out of my life.

Alcoholism wasn't the cause of my mother's estrangement, but it kept Chessie from finding a place in our lives. Seven years after cutting contact with Chessie, once she was pregnant with me, my mother attempted a reconciliation. There are photos of my maternal grandmother holding me in the hospital, then again three years later, sitting with me on our blue-and-white floral sofa. Chessie wears thick black-framed glasses. Her face is lined and dotted with age spots. Her hair, dyed a fiery orange red, hints at her tragic youth. I'm in a red dress and white tights, smiling at a woman I remember meeting once.

I was in middle school when Chessie died. My aunt and uncle tossed her hoarded possessions into a dumpster and brought anything salvageable to our house for an estate sale. My mother sorted Chessie's jewelry while I watched, appreciating a charm bracelet with tiny gold figurines. This wasn't real gold, my mother told me. But she didn't want to get rid of it. She also kept clothing, furs, black-and-white photos of her parents courting, and envelopes of love letters from my grandfather's time in the military. It was the stuff of Hollywood, pining letters from an abandoned wife to a man fighting for his county. *You should write a novel with these letters*, my mother suggested, finding a place for the love letters on a high closet shelf.

It took years to gather the courage to cut my father off.

Acting on advice from my mother and various therapists, I sent him letters detailing various slights. I was hurt and angry at being held to unspoken rules that only I had to follow. I couldn't visit a friend on one of "his" weekends, yet he thought nothing of going out with my stepmother and leaving me home alone, or ferrying my half brothers to various activities and clubs while insisting I stay with them for "family time," or calling me on my birthday to cancel a planned get-together in New York, where I'd moved after college. I hoped that if he knew how hurt I was, he'd want to treat me better.

At first, it seemed to work. We'd wind up apologizing for our respective actions and reach a shaky peace. I'd convince myself things would improve and let down my guard to give him a chance, only to wind up reeling when he lashed out in judgment, like blaming me for getting a flat tire the night before Thanksgiving—I hadn't been able to get it fixed in time for the holiday meal at his house. Although I was mentally and emotionally done trying to salvage a relationship, I went through the motions for my half brothers' sake.

Until the phone call that became the last straw, the year I turned thirty.

At my father's request, I'd organized a belated birthday dinner, dutifully booking a table at a restaurant we all enjoyed even though I didn't want to celebrate with them. Days before the dinner, he called to cancel because my youngest brother had a driver's ed appointment that same day. *He's not ready for his driver's test yet. It isn't even his last lesson*, I fumed, alternating between anger and tears. My needs were, once more, being dismissed as less important.

This seemingly ordinary incident showed me that I would always be held to a different standard from his other family. My behavior had to be flawless, while my half brothers were given the benefit of the doubt. I was relieved for their sake, but I could not ignore the growing anger that stiffened my spine. I, too, deserved better.

Admitting that my father could not love me unconditionally was crushing—I don't want to minimize the pain. But once I saw clearly what had always been true, I found resolve.

I would choose myself, and it would be enough.

Even though the decision brought peace, I struggled with shame and heavy grief. How could I explain a decision that most people would deem inconceivable or heartless? What kind of monster would people believe I was?

To avoid thinking, I kept busy, planting a vegetable garden surrounded by gladiolus bulbs. I put my faith in life, in newness, tending to my garden and, indirectly, to my heart.

My decision to cut contact reminded me of how it felt to finally come out as queer. I'd agonized over my coming out, spending years imagining friends' and relatives' shock and disgust when I told them the news, while simultaneously daydreaming about female crushes I was too shy to pursue.

Coming out wasn't easy, but it gave me immeasurable mental peace. It taught me to stop playing roles that did not fit for the comfort of others. It reminded me that other people did not need to understand my choice for it to be valid.

Chessie and Steven's love letters sit on a shelf in my mother's house. I've never read them; theirs isn't a love story that interests me. But over the years, writing has helped me nurture a connection to Chessie.

Chessie died at her kitchen table with a bottle in her hand. My mother had to go to the morgue and identify her body. To her, I imagine this provides justification for their decades of estrangement. Chessie was unwell; why would we want to be near that? Wasn't it safer for us that she remained a stranger? Hadn't my mother been a good parent by keeping us from her?

To me, her solitary death indicates a collective failing. Even though it's too late and not my responsibility, I find myself wanting to help Chessie. I have imagined alternate futures where Chessie has found support and healing from garden club members, bridge partners, new boyfriends, real estate colleagues, and her beloved pets. I have daydreamed pathways to healing for her because I, too, wanted to be healed of the pain of my choice. Envisioning supportive communities for Chessie has helped me focus on the support network I have, not the relationships I've lost.

Despite what cutting off my father might suggest, I am a loyal person. I've stayed connected with college friends, made new friends, and found a life partner who accepted me for who I was. Our wedding was joyful; less than a year after, we embarked upon a new adventure by moving from Boston to the Hudson Valley. I was reconnecting with nature, writing more, and settling into a confidence that came with giving up the performance.

There are sad days when I'm nostalgic for a happy, intact family of origin. Days when I feel deprived and judged for the toxic patterns within my family. Angry days when I resent my father, while understanding that men are not taught how to deal with their emotions constructively.

Like my parents' divorce, my extended family history has shaped me in ways I'm still exploring. While parts of the story are painful and the characters are certainly flawed, my female ancestors made bold choices to determine the shape of their lives. They lived for love and authenticity, with a desire for larger lives. Their boldness is also my legacy.

Wash Belly

Soni Brown

I watch my mother take in the unfamiliar mountain landscape of Provo, Utah, as we enter the clinic. "Is this Jamaica?" she asks. It's October 2018, and I'm regretting my hasty decision to bring her to live with me. Two days in, and I'm yelling at her for washing her hands in the toilet bowl. Two days in, and she calls me "Miss Lady." Two days in, and I wonder what I owe a woman who gave me scars but needs my healing now that her mind has emptied itself to the sky.

"I live eighty years of trial and tribulation. Nothing wrong with me except I can't hear so good," she tells me outside the free clinic, her words coming in jagged spurts, like she's spitting rocks.

But there is something wrong. The reports from my sister in Jamaica catalog it: getting lost on familiar paths; wandering late at night until villagers brought her home; inviting strangers to live in her house; emptying her bank account; threatening neighbors with machetes.

I look at her as she probably looked at her own mother when I was a baby. Forty years ago, Grandma was wandering the city streets mumbling to herself and eating out of rubbish bins. I wonder if my mother asked herself then as I do now how exactly one becomes unknown to herself. I recall stories of my grandmother abandoning Ma at three months. Grandma wanted to shed the yoke of rural life and become someone. She went to gallivant in Kingston, hosting salons for politicians. My mother grew up without her. They didn't connect until Grandma's body needed dressing for burial. This is my inheritance, this unraveling. This duty.

My mother and I are two women separated by more than oceans and continents. We are twin islands losing the landmarks that once defined us. She forgets her name, and I shed my accent. She loses her way home, and I refuse to call Jamaica home for decades. She is involuntarily lost from herself while I choose for my sanity not to connect with anything that reminds me of her.

I fled my mother's suffocating expectations of the old ways by using physical distance—the 1,690 miles between Kingston and Provo. The cultural divide is even worse. I rejected the obeah traditions to embrace an American life. There is the cognitive gulf now widening as dementia erases my mother's memories, transforming me from daughter to caretaker to stranger. And beneath it all runs a current of ancestral disconnection—the stories, customs, and knowledge that die with each forgotten name.

I was chosen for this vigil because of my estrangement. "It's your turn," my sister said, her voice delivering the fact always left unsaid. I'd spent the least amount of time with our mother. My siblings had their reasons for distancing themselves. My sister wanted freedom after financing our family. My farmer brother couldn't reconcile with our mother's cruelty. Two other brothers in Florida felt they'd sacrificed their youth as her surrogate husbands. As the youngest at forty, I was the "wash belly"—the last fruit of the family tree, the one meant to care for the parent. I'd been selected by my siblings to watch her die.

The clinic's waiting room screams faux cheer with its primary colors and fake plants. I watch my mother crouch by the window facing Provo's cemetery-cum-city-park. "Put Alzheimer's disease on that line," the receptionist says, slashing through my scrawled "cognitive impairment" on the intake form. He can see what I hadn't.

The land shapes us. Jamaica—lush, vibrant, demanding—forged my mother into a survivor. The mountains and valleys of her village taught her to be unyielding, to grow food from unforgiving soil, to weather hurricanes and droughts. Utah—sterile, ordered, alien—offers no such lessons. Here in Provo, with its grid system and temple spires, we are both displaced, uprooted from the fertile chaos that defined us.

Growing up in Kingston made me too sensitive. As a cure, I became my mother's unwilling apprentice in her world of whispered spells and spiritual rituals. By day, her words marked my place. "All gal children good for is to breed," she'd say while pouring resources into my brothers. I was a wife-in-training. By seven, I could scale and fry fish. By eight, I knew to bleach shirts whiter than holy. By nine, there was nothing my mother could do that I couldn't do myself.

Nights transformed her. The cold-cream smell as she slathered it on her face would draw me to her bedroom. Perched on her bed, I became not a future wife but a treasured consigliere.

She whispered obeah spells, taught me to commune with the dead and to sense evildoers' vibrations. I learned to brew ancestor-calling potions and plant money-summoning shrubs. She practiced openly what most hid in shadows. These illegal secrets made me a reluctant medium, split between living and binding to the dead.

For twenty years, I tried to outrun this legacy. I crossed oceans and remade myself, yet her influence clung to me like the persistent aroma of burning garbage.

My estrangement from her ran parallel to my rejection of my culture: They fed each other, creating concentric circles of disconnection. Rejecting my mother's spiritual practices meant rejecting the ancestors. Fleeing Jamaica meant leaving behind the land that shaped her worldview. Each choice to distance myself from her traditions widened the gulf between us, until we stood on opposite shores—she with her ancestral knowledge, me with my American reinvention.

Memory is like the sea. It ebbs and flows, erasing boundaries between seen and unseen, dredging hidden depths to the surface. At the clinic, my thoughts carry me back to the year I turned nine. Before this, I was the selectively mute child at a fancy prep school, taunted for having a mother who practiced obeah. "Boogie Girl," they called me. "Everything you touch is buggers." Their words lay inside me like lead until I stopped eating. When doctors and potions failed, my mother emptied her savings to consult a man more powerful than her ancient ways.

We arrived at his hut in the hills at dawn. My heart pounded. My palms slimed themselves with sweat. "Mama, please. Don't take me in there." She pushed me inside. A man's eyes reflected the smoke. His hands were instruments of menace. One hand clutched an ordinary kitchen knife, which in the dim light became an extension of his might.

I whispered, "He'll hurt me." But my mother—she who should have protected me—only turned and said, "Child, don't be ignorant. This is our way. This is what we do."

The bamboo door creaked shut behind her as she left. "You the vessel o' purity," he said as he began to remove my clothes, then his. I squeezed myself tight and imagined I was a duppy, a ghost who could board any Air Jamaica flight leaving the island with no intention of returning.

Is this where our estrangement began? Not with my physical departure at twenty but here, in this moment when protection became betrayal? When traditions became trauma? When my mother chose ancestral ways over my trembling body?

The doctor's voice cuts through my thoughts. "Physically, your mother seems fine," she says. "Her heart's holding up." The pause stretches. Each word falls like a stone as she continues. "We can't say it's Alzheimer's disease without a scan, but looking at her. Reading the symptoms. Her quality of life needs to be the focus."

I hear the rest in fragments.

"Advanced stage of dementia, for sure."

"Her speech will stop."

"Then walking."

"Maybe eating."

"Could live another ten years, maybe three."

The irony twists like a knife. My mother, who pressed stories into my ears with urgent insistence, "Don't forget," now forgets herself. The keeper of ancestral knowledge loses words like water through cupped hands.

As we exit the clinic, Ma's eyes sharpen. "Listen," she says. "*J-O-Y-C-E.* That's my name, but you call me Madge. Don't forget." Her fingers press into my arm.

We have both become strangers—she to herself, me to my roots.

In Provo's pallid sunlight so unlike the Caribbean heat, something shifts. As Ma stumbles, clinging to me, she whispers, "Don't leave, you hear." And I promise, "I won't, Ma."

I secure her seat belt like I do my toddler's. "Bless you, Miss Lady," she says. The words slice deep. A stranger again. But perhaps estrangement isn't permanent. Perhaps it's cyclical, like memory, like the sea.

We are adrift in this land of Mormons. I'm caught between Ma's forgetting and my reluctant remembering. I start the car. A prayer slips from my lips to whoever might be listening. Help me heal us both in the spaces between what's lost and what remains.

What Are the Chances?

Kristen Millares Young

Here's what it comes down to with Dad.

At the 2023 French Quarter Festival, in a city where neither of us live, I followed a writer friend through crowds. Eight hundred and fifty thousand people attend the festival. I can't say how many came to see Ani DiFranco that sunny Thursday. The grassy field was packed. My friend and I waited along the riverside to meet up with his partner. After Ani's set began, we found an opening in the eddying masses and began that do-si-do that all good concertgoers know.

This dance is an art set to music if you're doing it right. By angling your body in time to the beat, the waters part. Energy slips through the wave. People let you pass. My friend looked back occasionally. In the slightest clearing on the far side, we joined a countercurrent of folks flowing to the front, their single file hemmed in by a row of tented drink vendors. Trying to keep his backpack in sight, I merged into line directly in front of my father. I did one double take over my shoulder to affirm what I already knew. *Hey, Dad.*

Mouths do drop open. That's real. Beneath his straw hat, behind sunglasses, Dad's eyes grew wet. (Reader, please note: In my mind, before this happened, I'd resolved to begin calling my father by his first name, but that's not what I did.)

Four years into our ongoing estrangement, I bought myself time with gratuitous service, a move not unfamiliar to women. *Do you want a drink?* Beer for him, vodka soda for me. At the counter, the server talked about my hair, told me I was pretty. Behind her, the barkeeps were backed up. She began a guessing game about our ages. *Forty-one,* I said. *Proud of it, too . . . I've got a story if you want to hear it.*

Go for it, she said. *We've got time.*

My father and I haven't seen each other since 2019. We live on opposite sides of the country. And we just ran into each other in this crowd.

That's really something, she said. *At least you don't have to see him again if you don't want to.*

Drinks in hand, Dad and I decided to play it cool.

Between songs, I asked for backdated updates about the stepfamily. I filled him in about my children. We were both careful. He maddens me by containing multitudes. My father hides in plain sight. Who taught him that skill? How early did he learn? Our rivers braid from the same source.

Do we have to talk about it? Dad looked at the stage when asking the question. We both knew what *it* was.

Silence is your MO, right? A response to which he reacted as though I were indigestion.

It's not me he wants to see. He's long given up on me as a daughter. What he wants is to have influence over my kids. *We are going to have to talk*, I told him. He shook his head. I let it lapse.

My kin say things they don't mean when they're drinking. Later, they refuse to remember. They won't cop to the flicker in their eyes. In the realm of established narratives, the conversation never happened.

In fairness, they do the same when sober. Having failed to wring the truth from my family, I turned to distanced diplomacy. You could say I took the high road. I don't know where that is anymore. Might I have made a scene? Thrown something into his face for the edification of those around us?

Is that what I'm doing now?

After Ani wrapped up her set, Irma Thomas closed down the main stage with professional grace, and New Orleans put on a fireworks display. Most comfortable in the shallows, Dad put his arm around me. Gazing skyward, I didn't shake it off. Under this dark and glimmering sky, we performed like a loving family.

Together

Mattilda Bernstein Sycamore

When I was twelve, I decided I didn't respect my parents and I would never rely on them again. So I stopped telling them anything. They sent me to a therapist so the therapist would tell them what was going on. My parents were therapists, so I knew this was unethical. Luckily, my therapist would ask what I wanted him to tell them, and that's all he would say when they met once a month, and my parents were frustrated.

At first, I resented going to therapy, but then I kind of started to like it. Taking the bus across town after school, finding the fallout shelter in the basement with the cigarette machine and the corduroy sofa—it felt kind of sophisticated to be on my own.

I saw that therapist until I graduated from high school, once a week for six years, and I knew I couldn't tell him anything that was actually happening, so most of the time I made up dreams. He was a psychiatrist and a psychoanalyst, like my father, so he would nod his head and say how does that make you feel.

My parents thought I might be anorexic. I was anorexic, but of course I didn't tell him that. I said how could I be anorexic if I have all this energy. He said sometimes when you don't eat, it gives you energy. He had caught me, but I didn't let on. I also didn't mention the NoDoz or the Vivarin or hooking up with men in public bathrooms after class in high school.

After therapy, sometimes I would walk to Politics and Prose, the independent bookstore nearby, to wait for my father to pick me up and drive me home. I can't remember exactly what books I found there, but I know that by sixth grade, when I started therapy, I was reading *War and Peace* and *Crime and Punishment*. By the end of high school, I was reading Jean-Paul Sartre and thinking about freedom—this was what I was obsessed with, how trapped I felt by what I was supposed to be. Instead of studying all the time to go to a better college than anyone in my family so I could live in a bigger house and marry someone I hated just to prove that I wasn't a faggot, that I could win, that I could beat my father, I wanted to drop out and sip absinthe with Sartre on the Left Bank and talk about how doomed we all were.

Luckily, I did escape. When you escape, your life can truly begin, or that's how it felt. To live on your own terms means to live without your parents in mind, to reject their terms and everything about them, and that's what I did.

If you look at photos of me at twelve, I look like an incest survivor. I don't know how anyone missed this. Maybe they just pretended because I excelled at school. A year later, and I look like a different person. Because I realized I would never meet the people who would change my life if all I showed the world was fear. I had to start acting fearless, even if it was just an act.

Thirty years after my last session with my childhood therapist, I'm on my way to Politics and Prose again, to read from my new book, *Touching the Art*, about my relationship with my late grandmother, Gladys, who was an abstract artist. She nourished everything that made me different as a child and then tried to take that all back once my work and my world became avowedly queer. My work became vulgar to her, that was the word she would use. Why are you wasting your talent, she would say to me, over and over, for the last twenty years of her life, as we talked less and less.

Walking to Politics and Prose from the metro, I'm suddenly struck by memories I don't expect. Like the street where my high school was, or the street my literary magazine was named after. I'm on Connecticut, where my therapist was, walking past these grand apartment buildings like the one nearby where my other grandmother lived. I always loved her apartment, even if I couldn't stay. I mean I wanted to stay.

When I was twenty-one, I confronted my father about sexually abusing me. I gave him a fourteen-page document where I told him what I remembered, how the abuse had harmed me, how I was healing. I told him I would never speak to him again unless he could come to terms with it. He started screaming at me, he called me psychotic, and I walked away.

Eleven years later, he had acknowledged nothing, but I decided to visit him anyway because he was dying of cancer. I took the train cross-country. Sometimes strangers give you the best advice, and a stranger on the train, a nurse, told me that when someone is dying, on that morphine drip and unable to say much of anything, they can hear everything. They understand everything, she said, so say it all, don't hold anything back.

So I didn't hold anything back. I told him that I loved him, and I wished that we could have a relationship, even though I didn't know either of those things until I was standing at his deathbed, and I heard the sound of excitement he made when he said my name, and I started sobbing. I told him that he could still acknowledge sexually abusing me, that this could still change my life.

He acknowledged nothing. Still, this was one of the best decisions of my life, because I no longer needed to hold the trauma inside or pretend nothing was going on, like how I survived my childhood.

When I was working on *Touching the Art*, I started by literally touching Gladys's art to feel what would come through, and after writing dozens of pages about this experience, I went into my file cabinets to find the letters we exchanged when I was nineteen, twenty, twenty-one, twenty-two, just before and just after I confronted my father about sexually abusing me. I had photocopies of my letters as well, because at that time, after I remembered I was sexually abused, I didn't want to forget anything.

When I confronted my father and sent the same letter I gave him to my four grandparents, Gladys called me up and said: If this is true, how do I go on living?

At the time I thought this was an honest response, but now I realize it was just another way of pressuring me to lie. Reading over her letters, I see that she's accusing me of hurting the family by confronting my father. I'm the one causing the harm.

This was something I didn't remember at all. I mean I remembered that she refused to support me, like everyone else in the family, that she supported the lie of the family over my life, but I didn't remember she was so brazen in her accusations, insisting that I consider "all sides" to the story, as if there can be two sides to a father raping his child. "We all want to get on with our lives," she wrote, as if I was in the way.

When I was working on *Touching the Art*, I interviewed anyone who knew Gladys, and that meant talking to relatives I'd only spoken to years before, or sometimes relatives I had never met. Almost everyone wanted to talk to me, they wanted to share what they knew. One cousin sent me a video her daughter made of a visit from Gladys to her seventh-grade class, another cousin sent me a video she made at age fifteen when visiting Gladys's house, and several sent me photos of Gladys's paintings that she gave to them.

When I was a kid, I didn't know many members of my extended family. We would go to my cousins' house nearby in the DC suburbs for Passover every year. I looked forward to visiting them because I liked the whole celebration, from singing the prayers to searching for the afikomen and waiting for Elijah. I bonded especially with Kim and Claire, older cousins I barely knew, but I would get hints of our mutual curiosity from a shared glance or a giggle. Once or twice, we went over for Rosh Hashanah too, but then my mother didn't want to go anymore, so that was the end. There weren't many visits aside from that.

While working on the book, I had several conversations with my mother, both on the phone and in person at her place in DC with Gladys's art all around us. She told me things I never knew—for example, when I was less than two years old, she was worried something was wrong because I liked ribbons and women's fashion magazines, and Gladys would take me into her bed and call me a pretty boy. So my parents took me to a therapist, who didn't think there was a problem.

Don't you think the real problem was your homophobia, I said.

I wouldn't call it homophobia, my mother said.

What about when I came out to you and you suggested that I go to conversion therapy?

I wouldn't call it homophobic. I wanted you to have an easier life.

But then, when I finished the manuscript, I read her all the parts where I included our conversations or wrote about my father's abuse, and she surprised me when her only complaint was that she wanted me to read the whole book to her.

So in a way, I became closer to her, and to other relatives, by writing about all the ruptures in my relationship with Gladys. The ruptures in the family.

When you start a reading, you walk into the room. When you walk into the room, you feel it, what's there for you. All the energy in the room.

Don't get me wrong, the first question after I read at Politics and Prose was: Do you think you would still be queer if it weren't for the abuse? Don't worry, I knew how to handle that nonsense, but what was important was the energy in the room, with such a diverse crowd—all ages, standing room only, everyone wearing masks because I requested it. Some people think masks make the room less intimate, but to me we're closer because we're taking care of one another. There was a blond woman in the audience who watched me closely with tears in her eyes when I was talking about being sexually abused, so I figured she was a survivor too.

But afterward, during the signing, was when it all came together. Someone from my class in high school came up—we hadn't seen each other since we graduated. Someone else, living just down the street in her father's house after he died. And then the blond woman came up with another woman. They said, do you remember us?

I didn't recognize them until they said it's Claire and Kim. Cousins I hadn't seen since childhood Passovers. They were both seven years older than me—when you're a kid, that's a lot, but when you're fifty, it's nothing.

After a reading is when I feel the most alive. All the vulnerability and connection, the openness. It's what I write toward. And when it's met, I feel like a different person.

I had invited Kim to the reading, but when I didn't hear back, I assumed she wouldn't be there. And now here she was with Claire.

Kim had told me that my mother had refused to give them my contact info. I didn't even know they kept asking for it. But now here we were, together again after thirty-five years.

They asked what I was doing after the reading.

Do you want to go on a walk, I said.

And so we did.

Pattern Recognition

Oslyn Serratos

Around six years old, I decided that I could construct my own sense of self, just like a LEGO set. Everything would be okay if I could just put together the right blocks in the right pattern. A Goody Two-shoes, chatty and precocious, a voracious reader who loved to perform, I imagined myself as a colorful set of tiles that could be rearranged, popping out any pieces I didn't like. I was confident I could always remake myself.

But my father and I were competing architects in the construction of my adolescent identity. "I made you. I know who you are," my dad would say in a smooth, dismissive voice, his back straight from years in the Air Force. If I liked a movie or a joke or a person he didn't like, he'd say I only did it to be rebellious. My mother and my younger brother had long since realized that conflict could be avoided if they agreed with him or, better, said nothing. Fathers aren't usually questioned in Brown immigrant families, but I've never been good at falling in line.

I didn't understand why he and I were locked in this battle until one night, after another tearful (on my part) fight about me refusing to apologize for something I hadn't done. "You're manipulative," my dad said in a soft, comforting tone, sitting next to me on my bed in our suburban house. "I'm hard on you because I'm afraid you're becoming a psychopath. I have to make you feel the right things. Your mom doesn't see it, but I do."

He meant it as our little secret, like he was only trying to help me, but I felt it as a lie—or maybe as a truth that was more about him than me. I couldn't stop seeing all the untruths that contradicted the loving father we both believed he was. The pattern didn't hold.

At night I would go over my memories, weighing them against all the little lies he told, usually about how someone—often me—had wronged him. In our family, facts were determined by who could win the argument, so it was important to never be wrong. It was no use asking my brother or mom for backup. *If that's what you remember, then you tell Dad*, my brother would respond. *I'm not taking the blame*, my mom would say.

My dad had been teased for not being able to speak English when he immigrated from Mexico during middle school. His teenage sisters had raised him, the last of twelve kids all jockeying for attention from disinterested parents. Even now, his greatest fear is that we'll see he's still that insecure boy. His favorite trick is sleight of hand. Instead of hiding coins, he deflects responsibility. My mom is the magician's assistant. No matter how badly the trick fails, she instructs us to clap. It took me over twenty years to realize that her actions were also a form of abandonment.

When I was growing up, my father had the authority of God. As Christians who were "in this world but not of this world," my parents didn't believe in politics or other outside influences. God was over the country and Dad was over the family. We even stopped going to church because he could preach to us himself. My brother and I grew up socially isolated, homeschooled until middle school. We were each other's only friend and classmate, bonding over make-believe and cultural references only we shared. Four years younger, he followed me everywhere, slept in my bed when he was scared. But we competed to be the "good one" in a home where the rules didn't have to make sense as long as they aligned with our Dad's top-down morality. On one hand, I was winning: My academic achievements made my parents look good. On the other hand, I became the scapegoat for resisting the family dynamic. She who spotted the fallacies, caused the drama.

Sometimes I didn't have enough experience to spot the lie my intuition felt. Dad claimed he was the only one who would tell us the real truth. Truth like: *Your mother didn't want you when she was pregnant, but I saved you from abortion.* Or, when I wondered if I was depressed: *You're supposed to feel like that; everyone does.* And: *I'm only telling you this because I love you; I'm only telling you what no one else will.* It's hard to put a puzzle together when you can't find the edges.

"You shouldn't trust sisters," I overheard my dad tell my brother once in a conspiratorial tone meant to divide and conquer—private conversations managed the balance of power. I wasn't surprised: According to the Bible, I had inherited Eve's deception. I guess that lesson stuck with my brother. He started to pull away as we grew older, first from me and then, eventually, from everyone in our family.

"We just don't know if we can trust you around our daughter," my brother said during our last phone call. "We have standards." To him, families run on authoritarianism, so my happy home feels out of control. My husband and I both manage community service programs, and there is no head of the house. We carry the workload together and raise our kids to be kind, accountable, and unafraid to get messy.

As a child, my brother had been the family comedian, but he grew from jovial and mischievous to stoic and terse. "Always address me and my wife when you call. We're a unit," he instructed in that last conversation. "You don't take your marriage seriously like we do." That was laughable—I would have to inform my husband of fourteen years. "We're going to make sure our kids are always in sports. We're not going to let them be lazy like yours," he continued. Like my parents, he fears idle hands and extra pounds, instead seeing physical fitness as a sign of discipline and success.

If I see myself as a set of multicolored blocks, then my brother is a straight line—just the way he used to arrange his toys—still following the same path we inherited. Hearing him talk, I realized that attempting to fix our relationship was futile.

"Grow up," he said then. My brother always speaks like an angry coach. "We aren't kids on the playground. 'Siblings' doesn't mean anything now that we have our own families." I rolled my eyes. That was news to me, but I'd been to enough therapy to know how to draw a line.

"I guess we don't need to do this anymore," I said. Resignation felt like both failure and freedom.

As I hung up, my whole body started to shiver, and the tears came with deep gasps that made it hard to breathe. My husband put his arms around me as I shook—he's seen me like this before; it's not the first time my family has threatened to disown me. My parents tried it a few times until they realized I wasn't going to apologize. It never sticks, but it always hurts. When my eyes dry, there is a lightness, like having shed a piece that no longer fits.

Most days, I forget I even have a brother. We had been strangers for years prior to this phone call—I'm not mourning the relationship we had, more the loss of our shared childhood and what could have been, if we didn't live in different realities. But to see him fade from being my kids' godfather to not even acknowledging them on birthdays and holidays is a wound that might not close. I'm glad they are still young enough to forget. I won't teach them to love a ghost.

My parents don't know why my brother barely talks to them. They prayed, and God said it wasn't their fault—how *very* specific of God. It's easier to see myself without siblings than without parents—the only links to my past and my cultures. We are each other's only family, and my LEGO set doesn't make sense without that foundation. My parents and I are not physically estranged, but emotionally, we've been cut off from each other for over a decade. They just don't know it. Our time spent together is half me gray rocking, sticking to neutral topics like the kids, weather, gossip, and half them not wanting to know a truth they can't handle. I see them every weekend, so my kids can have grandparents who pretend to be what I always wanted. I hope this new shape of our relationship, not quite parent and child, can last. It helps that I don't hold out much hope. I remind my inner child that she's grown now. She doesn't need them; she has me.

Recently, I took a risk over the phone and told my parents I was diagnosed with ADHD—all the blocks were clicking into place now.

"I knew you never had any discipline," my father spat, like

he'd been waiting to say this for thirty years. "You could never follow through or finish anything you started. You couldn't train your dog, or your horse, or your bird. I tried to teach you discipline, but you wouldn't learn. Just like you wouldn't learn Spanish."

All the baby animals he'd purchased before I was even twelve—no shit a kid wasn't able to train them on her own. I just laughed and reminded him of his litany of failed careers and false starts. And *he* was the little boy ashamed to speak Spanish, but he's forgotten that now.

My mom was holding the phone; he was yelling from somewhere in the background. You could never call just one of them. The other is always listening, questioning why you didn't ask for them first—just like my brother and his wife.

"I knew you couldn't clean your room properly when you were young," my mom said matter-of-factly. "I think you're just lazy. You want to take the easy way out with medication. If you changed your diet and lost weight . . ." My parents are always on a diet, one of the few things they can still control.

I know their conspiracies about mental health and the loss of traditional values are the result of generational trauma and their obsession with Fox News. Yet I feel a deep sadness for my parents who see but don't understand why our worldviews don't align. My own hurt feels disassociated, like it's happening to someone else, maybe the daughter they wanted me to be, but not who I actually am.

With this foundation, my brother and I never had a real chance. Like our parents, he takes comfort in believing he is better than others—better than me. My brother won't return my parents' calls, but at least he still goes to church. At least he still has traditional beliefs. At least he's not fat. A prodigal son is better than a jezebel daughter.

Good thing ADHD correlates with high pattern recognition. It wasn't hard for me to see that the pieces don't add up. That their conservative values don't match up with the love that Christians preach. That the beautiful parts that made us feel like a close family—road trips where we drove all night eating snacks; camping at Lake Tahoe; talking about books after walks to the library—don't add up with the ugly ones that made me question everything. That the moments I thought were special—like parents confiding in me in a way that made me feel so grown up as a child—now seem misshapen in retrospect. If I don't match all the pieces just right, it's pretty easy to get lost in the mess. I'm not surprised my brother chose to surrender rather than sift through it all.

Now, my reality is built on hard truths and broken cycles—a new pattern for the future. Looking around at my kids, at our home in a waterfront city, I like what I am. In therapy and through writing, I took myself apart to find the proof that I am worthy. Reassembled, I realize there is no right way to be. Whatever shape I am is just fine.

A Sister's Salve

Danielle Jernigan

I've come to a place in my life where I can sleep through the night. Mornings are slow and peaceful. My five-year-old, Zoë, and I greet each other with a zerbert kiss, cuddling under the blanket. I eventually sign "good morning" because she is both nonspeaking and autistic; sometimes she signs back. We enjoy a gentle yoga flow, which often feels more like a game of Twister but that doesn't matter to me. Her smile and giggle awaken in me a deep longing to know what naivety and safety would have felt like at her age.

Today is the anniversary of my birth. I've made forty-nine trips around the sun, and thanks to social media, everyone who is a friend of a friend is wishing me happiness and joy on this blessed day. The consideration makes me smile. I rarely give much thought to my birthday, as it isn't something I remember my parents celebrating. I am basking in the warmth of these thoughtful messages when I receive a text from my sister.

"Dad called *again* to make sure I told you happy birthday."

A heavy tightness settles at the base of my neck, casting a shadow over the joy. I believe my sister means no harm. She has taken the role of mediator and messenger in our family, seeking to keep us all up-to-date on the good and bad of our many branches spanning states and generations. Yet her commitment to this role makes the task of enforcing my boundaries much more difficult and requires a certain finesse to preserve my most important relationship: the one I have with myself.

A tug of wills ensues between my head and heart. My head is rational, but my heart speaks to the possibility of change. Do I go back on my promise to myself? Or do I take the risk of alienating my sister by demanding my boundaries be respected? I already feel alone in my family. Their religion says that I should honor my mother and father so my days on earth will be long. Do I take the risk of shortening my tenure here and leaving Zoë prematurely? Do I even believe the threat? What about the scripture that admonishes parents not to provoke their children to wrath?

My wrath has been sacred—like a willow in the wind, bending and swaying with quiet tension, until the storm hits and it snaps back with a force that shatters the calm. I have not spoken to my father in more than ten years, outside of a cordial "Hello" or the obligatory "My children are fine." The last time I physically saw him was at the annual family barbecue. Zoë was six months old, and my aunt Anna, my father's sister, had invited us.

There my father sat, under a towering tree in the front yard, with a beer and cigarette in hand. Just like old times. Seeing me with Zoë on my hip, his eyes lit up and with a smile, he made his way over to me. His large calloused right hand patted his upper thigh as if to help him keep a rhythm and not stumble—always an indicator of his intoxication level. Dressed in his signature Kangol hat, button-up short-sleeve shirt, and jeans, my father was the same man I'd known as a young girl, yet his face was softer than I remembered. I reluctantly let him hug me and speak to his granddaughter. He attempted to take her from my arms, sensed me tighten my grip, and with one look from me, realized he'd better not.

As I turned to enter the house, the familiar lump rose in my throat. My stomach flipped and the dark cloud of guilt began to gather over my head. The only way to avoid its downpour was to dissociate from my body for a moment, to hover just beyond the edge of sound and feeling, above the mingling relatives in the front yard, becoming more observer than participant.

It used to take me weeks after these encounters to come back into my body, but as of late I practice embodiment, make space for stillness, allow the emotional turmoil to rise and stabilize. I recognize I have the right to expect that my family honor my choices. But the shouldas come anyway: I should be past this. In my fiftieth year of living, I should be able to stand tall, say my piece, and not give two cents about what others think. I *should* forgive.

My sister is six years younger than me. Born on the first day of spring, she embodies Piscean energy: gentle, perceptive, once unanchored. Now that she is a studied ordained minister, that same sensitivity has become her strength. She believes that everyone should be forgiven, especially our parents. At least, this is what I infer. We've never had this conversation.

For my sister, our father was merely a hardworking functional alcoholic who was absent from her life due to divorce. I speculate it's easier for her to forgive him. From my vantage point, forgiveness feels elusive. I may never reach it, and I have made my peace with that.

Growing up in a home full of violence and chaos, you learn to expect your everyday life will be riddled with fear. It's the kind of fear that you need to be in touch with so you stay alive. Fear was my protector. It kept me ready and my eyes open. But fear was also a mischievous thief who stole bits of my life, dampened the good memories with the bad, claiming to save me from myself.

In my imperfect memory, my sister's early years are fleeting—flashes of time solidified by found photos, VHS home movies viewed at the annual Christmas party, and puzzled recollections of extended family. Though the memories of our shared moments are scattered, the only place we lived together with my father is etched much more clearly in my mind: a green plantation-style house at the top of a hill, behind which the Indian River carved a path after rushing over the dam. I used to play along its banks, rolling down the hill in cardboard boxes, catching fish, and skipping stones. At the top of the hill, on the other side of a wooden fence with gaps so big we could climb between, stood a grand weeping willow, its roots deep in the earth. On restless nights, I cracked my window to listen to the river sing to the willow, its rhythm soothing the tension that filled the house and my little body.

Outside the green house, my sister would join me on my nature explorations: We'd make mud pies, pick baby crabs from the river, or explore the neighbor's magnolia tree adorned with bright white blooms and stamens that looked like matchsticks.

My sister doesn't remember any of this, but she still blames me for her fear of cats because the old neighborhood tabby scratched her under my watch. What I know for sure is that I never left her in that house alone with our father.

My parents fought—no, they battled. Always quietly, sometimes violently. I'd wake after a night of little to no sleep and creep down the stairs, listening, hoping the smoke had cleared. The air inside was thick like in those old war movies, gray with the aftermath. We acted as if it were normal to see broken glass and spilled gin on the hardwood floors or holes in the walls from where my mother had thrown yet another pan. They'd clean it up to the sound of Prince or Hall & Oates on the stereo, which was my sign that danger was over.

Sometimes, if our mother picked up a weekend shift, I bore the brunt of my father's wrath. If the afternoon was too hot or rainy to play outside, I'd sit stiff on the couch, pretending to watch *Star Trek* or whatever Western he had on, waiting for Mr. Hyde to emerge. As my father sipped beer then chased it with a swig of Seagram's and a drag off his Salem, the mumbling would start, the teeth grinding—markers that the transformation into a monster had begun, full of rage at everyone and everything but mostly at me.

The sound of it—that low, relentless grating—needled its way into my skin, summoning tears I dared not shed. I fought to hold them back knowing that one small slip would set him off. One such day, he commanded me to get a paper towel from the kitchen. Instead, I headed toward the stairs, hoping to hide in the bathroom. He grabbed my arm and hurled me toward the kitchen. As I passed the red phone on the wall—the one I'd run to many times to call 911 but never had the courage to dial—I wiped my face slowly, deliberately stalling my return to the living room. When I entered the hallway, my face met his hard calloused fist. He knocked me flat on the cold wooden floor. I looked up at the phone and thought, if I could just call someone—someone to help me, to help us. But there was no one to call. Not even my mother.

The sun going down did not signal a time of rest for a hypervigilant child. I'd lie in bed listening for the familiar creak of my father's footsteps at my door. Facing the open window, I tried to soothe myself with the sound of the river, meditating to its steady flow and watching the willow's branches dance to its rhythm. Sometimes I'd doze off but often I stayed awake until sunrise. Some nights, my father would pause then mercifully turn from my door. But not always.

Terror has a scent: beer hops, the pine of gin, and Salem cigarettes. Its aroma made me curl into a fetal position, clasp my hands between my legs, and pray to a God who never seemed to listen. If He was truly omnipresent, how could He watch what would happen next?

Through the years, I tried to tell many people about my father's abuse. Once, an aunt said nothing as she witnessed my father throw me to the ground and punch me in the chest for having had an altercation with a girl in school. I told another aunt why I didn't wish to see my parents, and she dismissed my father's contribution. "Your mom had issues, too—just pray about it," she said. I wrote letters to my mother. I shared with my third-grade teacher how afraid I was of my father. My mother never responded to my letters. My teacher patted me on the back and said, "I'm sorry, dear. Go back to your seat."

Our family, like most families riddled with abuse, addiction, and unresolved trauma, ignored problems. Our mantras included "Everyone goes through something," "God doesn't give you more than you can bear," or "Girl, it ain't that bad. Stop crying." This was the one I heard from my mother the only evening I ever ran to her for safety when my father was in a rage.

My mother eventually left my father the summer before I entered junior high. That evening, my sister and I jumped in the red hatchback and squeezed in beside the plastic laundry baskets full of our stuff. As we pulled away, my father stood on the porch of our green house and gave my mother the middle finger. My sister cried, and I imagined what life might become without the torment. As we drove away, I had never felt so vindicated—until my mother married a drug dealer who was just as abusive to her. He never touched my sister or me, but the life he lived did not yield a stable home, unlike the strange consistency and shelter that my father and mother had provided.

We moved from place to place, living out of hotels, drifting without roots. Eventually, my sister and I were parceled out—to an aunt here, a cousin there—scattered like pieces of someone else's burden. We were like the Israelites after their exodus from Egypt: freed but not settled; wandering in the wilderness, waiting for a Moses who never came. By the time I reached my junior year, I had attended two middle schools and three high schools. I felt abandoned—first by my mother, then by God. The same cycles kept looping around me. Cycles of abuse. Cycles of absence. I hated God. I hated my father even more. I stopped feeling sorry for my mother.

As a young girl, I knew there were two things I must do: survive and protect my little sister from the contamination of abuse. A stabilizing force in my life, like the willow tree by our old house, she gave me a sense of all that is beautiful and untainted. I never let her out of my sight or my mind's eye if we weren't physically together. Whenever we lived in the same home, she'd sleep in my bed, climbing in behind me, and I'd lay with my back to hers, facing the door and listening for footsteps. My instincts were a blend of moral, maternal, and animal. It was my duty to preserve her innocence.

The years we spent bouncing between homes and schools, aunties and uncles, brought me closer to my sister than ever before. Because of my constant thoughts of her, making sure she brushed her teeth, walking her to the bus, keeping her safe above all, I believed an unspoken loyalty and understanding existed between us. Our roots were deep and intertwined, anchoring us to each other when storms would rage.

At seventeen, pregnant, I moved in with the father of my son, but I was never far from my sister. If girls bothered her at school, I'd show up for her. Later, if the father of her children or our mother caused drama, I'd answer her call. We partied together. We hated each other. We loved each other. We were sisters. When my son was eight years old, I graduated from college and moved to the Midwest, away from the demons and the memories. While my sister and I kept in contact via phone, sharing the ups and downs of our lives, our conversations skimmed the surface—almost perfunctory. I would learn years later during a heated argument that she had felt abandoned; my guilt became a wound that never quite healed.

Yet my pilgrimage away from home was necessary. Away from family, I could see how enmeshed we had been in our dysfunctions. Free from them, I became an ambitious go-getter, earning degrees, going off to medical school, coauthoring scientific manuscripts and textbooks, and traveling the world. But cycles of depression and an eventual suicide attempt landed me in intensive outpatient therapy. I had not talked to my father in years, although my sister kept me informed of the events of his life. For the first time, in the safety of group therapy, the rage I had suppressed toward him began to surface.

I don't know what made me call my father that spring morning a year later, but I knew it was time. A few months earlier, I had returned to Delaware from the Midwest—reluctantly—for a job offer at an East Coast university.

That morning, I sat across the street from my small apartment on a swinging bench in the lush garden, basking in the sun. I thought about the irony of returning to the place I was born—and in some aspects always hated—and about the last thing my therapist told me: *Don't stop the work you've begun.* As I dialed the number, my hands shook, my chest tightened, and I recognized the familiar fear—ever present and keeping me at the ready.

"Hey, Ladybug," he answered.

I tried hard not to cry but couldn't contain it any longer. "I remember everything you ever did to me. Everything."

He paused. "Well, everyone goes through something in life. But I love you."

"You call that love?" I asked.

"You're right," he said. "I was an angry man. I wasn't able to love you. But I do now."

There it was. The validation of a truth I had known in my

bones all my life: My father had not loved me. I had spent years trying to rationalize his behavior, making excuses for him, and believing there was something to be saved. But with his confession, I could finally free myself from the guilt of being a daughter who struggled to honor him, a daughter who didn't want to know him.

Why wasn't this the case with my sister? She wanted a relationship with our father because he had been so absent in her life after our parents' divorce. She believed that our mother had kept him from us. So she pursued him. The person she came to know was not the monster I had experienced. And I believe that she wanted me to know the version of him she saw, to grow to forgive that man.

But I couldn't continue to subject myself to such torture. Instead of coming to family events, I began to avoid them altogether.

Each time my sister sends me a message about our father, I'm jolted back to a time I don't want to remember. I'm angered by what I perceive as her disloyalty, what I believe she owes me. And still, I experience this primal hurt when my father won't take the time to call me to say happy birthday himself, to ask about my children, to get to know me—even if I won't answer.

For my sister, forgiveness means a relationship. Family means loyalty—no matter what. As a minister and disciple of God, she seems to feel an obligation to work toward forgiveness and to rebuild relationships. For me, loyalty is earned, and I don't believe in blind forgiveness for the transgressions I experienced at the hands of my father. I live with the memories, I dream them, they haunt me, and while the dreams have become less frequent, my father remains a real-life monster. He still sits on the edge of my bed.

My father never showed me love because he didn't have the capacity to give it. At this point in my life, I vacillate between righteous anger and an eerie sense of compassion toward him. Yet I do not care to have him in my life. Even in his pursuit of me through messages to my sister, I don't sense any accountability. He has never said "I'm sorry." If he did, I am not sure it would matter.

"Dad called *again* to make sure I told you happy birthday."

It took me two days to summon the courage to send my sister a voice memo asking her once again not to convey messages from my father to me.

I paused before responding. I thought about my sister and my daughter. I thought about myself. My father had decimated my soul, wounded me in a way that forever changed me. The only tool I had left to honor myself was my voice. To create a different emotional inheritance for my daughter, I had to risk it all—even breaking the root binding me to my sister, the person I loved most beyond my children and myself.

I knew that in upholding my boundaries, there was a high probability I could lose my sister or transform our relationship to a shell of itself. But this decision was bigger than our relationship. This choice would impact my maternal legacy. I now had a daughter who had become the medicine, like an ancient salve made from the bark of a willow tree that had healed me. If I did not take this chance to use my voice, to solidify the growth I had achieved, how could I help Zoë cultivate hers? How would I continue to grow into the model I wanted for her?

As I sent my voice memo, I could imagine the dissonance my sister must feel as a believer of God and his scripture, as both a daughter and a sister. I imagined she thought I would go to hell for failing to reconcile with our father. Over the years she may have been confused by my sometimes-weak boundaries—inviting him to my son's high school graduation or tolerating pictures she'd take of us at occasional family events. She likely felt torn about whether to tell him that I didn't want to hear from him. My heart wept for her struggle and for mine.

"Okay," she replied.

She stopped responding to my messages and calls for months. Her silence hurt. Her rejection. This depth of betrayal. This was the sister I had protected and whom I would defend against all enemies, including our father. My sister could reciprocate this protection by acknowledging my pain and the truth of our family dynamic. She could attempt to perceive him through my eyes and choose not to shroud our estrangement in biblical anecdotes to defend the person who had crippled me.

But here is the thing: We are all on our own path. Perception is our only reality, and only in the house of time do we come to understand what we had not. Did my sister really have to see our father as I did to preserve our relationship? Maybe instead, this voice memo was the call to shape-shift our relationship into something more honest, to banish hidden secrets and thoughts unspoken. Maybe it was the call to unravel our roots, clean the rot from them, and move them toward new soil, fresher water. Maybe, because family is everything to her, my sister would finally do the work to understand me. And we could achieve a state of peace with each other, maybe in time become closer than ever.

—

I've reached the point in my life where I can sleep through the night. I've learned to be present with and for my children and myself. Our home is warm and our days are filled with hugs and celebrations when Zoë uses her voice. My daughter is the full expression of herself, a grounding presence in my life, a reminder of life's promise of renewal and transformation. She's safe and so am I—I, too, am working on being the full expression of myself.

Present/Tense

Susan Ito

My birth mother and I began our first estrangement on the day I was born. She claims that I was removed from her body while she was in "twilight sleep." This form of anesthesia, popular in the 1950s and '60s, dulled pain awareness as well as dimmed the memory of pain. We both remained hospitalized, in separate spaces; she for a lingering infection and me because I was premature and underweight. But eventually, she recovered and I grew enough to be discharged. She held me in a taxi where we were face-to-face for the first time. Reportedly, she fed me from a bottle on the way to the adoption agency. Then she returned to her home hundreds of miles away, and I was sent to a "boarding mother," or foster home. Six weeks later, I was adopted by my Japanese American parents and grew up as their beloved only child—finally, a half Japanese baby had become available after ten years on the agency's waiting list.

This initial period of estrangement from my birth mother lasted for twenty years, until I was a college student searching for answers, identity, history. I knew only that this invisible mother had been Japanese and my father was not. I chafed every time someone asked me, "What's your other half?" and I had no answer.

We remet for the first time in a generic hotel room. The moment that the door opened, I was struck that she was the same height as me, with familiar round cheeks and lips. I thought she was beautiful. But she was ambivalent, wary, and angry at having her privacy betrayed. "This wasn't supposed to happen," she said tersely. Apparently, the adoption agency had promised her anonymity forever. I was simultaneously smitten and intimidated. All I had to offer was an envelope of childhood photos, images from the years we had been apart. As she shuffled through pictures of me in a kimono in front of a Christmas tree, splashing in a Fred Flintstone floatie in Miami Beach, wearing a Brownie uniform, she gradually softened, and a fragile connection began. We became secret pen-pals, and I was giddy when I opened an envelope with her familiar, perfect cursive. She wanted to stay in touch, but it was to be a secret between us. She told me she wasn't ready to tell my half siblings about me, nor anyone else in her life.

The first Christmas that we were in contact, she surprised me by sending a hand-stitched miniature pillow ornament. The small, plump rectangle centered the words YOU ARE SPECIAL spelled out in tiny pink *X*'s, with my name on the back. I cradled it in my palm, murmuring the words out loud. *You are special.* After her initial suspicion and anger, this message meant everything.

She was in town for business later that year and agreed to meet my adoptive parents and grandmother. We dined together on Mother's Day at a Japanese sushi restaurant, and I was shocked at how well they all got along. They shared a culture and heritage as well as parentage of me.

The following Christmas, I received a red satin heart ornament. On my birthday, she often sent multiple gifts, perhaps making up for birthdays past. Maybe I *was* special. A soft waffle-weave nightshirt. A pair of director's chairs when I got my first apartment. An egg separator (the irony did not escape me) and other gadgets for my new kitchen.

I sent gifts to her too. I heard her mention the flowers that evoked her childhood and delivered her tulip bouquets. Her favorite, one that always elicited an enthusiastic thanks, was special assorted chocolates wrapped in white paper. I sent boxes for her birthday, for Mother's Day, and other holidays. I would have done anything to make her happy—except, perhaps, stop asking questions.

As the years went by, I began to get restless with the secrecy and my many unanswered questions. Who was my father? Would I ever be able to be "out of the closet" about this relationship? Would she tell my half siblings about my existence? As I started asking more questions, fissures grew between us and gradually, the letters and gifts stopped coming. Fifteen years into our reestablished relationship, I crossed a line. By this time I had married and had two daughters. I opened the question of my birth father again. I had done some investigating on my own, and I told her some of the hints I'd found. I asked if I was on the right track. After an angry response—something along the lines of "How dare you!"—she cut off all contact.

One of the last ornaments I'd received from her was a miniature version of the Queen of Hearts, sternly pointing a finger. I could hear the caption, "Off with her head!" and felt my own neck close to the chopping block.

This rupture almost broke me. It was one thing to be relinquished as an infant. I had been just an idea at that point—a future human, not yet a whole person. But now we had accumulated years of visits, of correspondence, of phone calls, and what had felt like a true connection. She had slept on the sofa in my studio apartment, and we'd eaten at what became our favorite Moroccan restaurant, sitting on the floor and eating couscous with our fingers. I had met up with her in hotels, in airports, in restaurants. We had exchanged souvenirs and snacks. She had even come to my wedding. To be ghosted at this point in our relationship was excruciating.

At Christmas time, I unwrapped the ornaments from their tissue-paper nests: the red satin heart, the YOU ARE SPECIAL pillow. It was an exquisite form of torture to hang them on my tree, but I felt compelled to remind myself, by holding these small tangible gifts in my hands, that once it had been true. Once, I had been special. Once, she had given me a heart.

I asked myself: If the person who had brought me into this world didn't want anything to do with me, should I even exist? My beloved husband and children brought me back from the edge more than once, and I found some healing by learning Japanese taiko drumming. To strike the enormous drums with thick wooden drumsticks, to shout and move around them, released all the emotion that had burned inside me. My sensei taught us that taiko echoed the sound of a mother's heartbeat in the womb. Eventually, I learned to live without her again.

I didn't hear from her for over six years. And then, unexpectedly, she reappeared. I received a letter where she said she didn't want to hold on to anger anymore.

Our connection had lost the warmth and ease of our earlier years—she never again signed a letter with "Love," and I never received another ornament or other gift. The nightshirt she had given me years before had worn down into a dustrag. But still, it was something. We transitioned from snail-mail cards and postcards to email. A few times over a decade, we arranged to get together for a meal. I always experienced the same spark and flutter from our first meeting, the thrill of any small connection. We posed for selfies, smiling. We still shared a bond in spite of everything. It kept me hoping for a growing closeness.

I never gave up wanting to know about my birth father but knew better than to persist in asking her more questions. Through the use of consumer DNA technology, I finally located his family, forty years after my birth mother and I first met. After four decades of wondering and asking, I learned he had died three years prior. But his sister, my genetic aunt, welcomed me with unabashed love and open arms. Her first words to me were "Welcome to the family!" I was startled to see that we shared the same nose, the same curve of the cheek. When I flew to meet her for the first time, I had hoped that she and I might visit with my birth mother, who lived within driving distance. I brought two boxes of her favorite chocolates. But my mother adamantly refused. She wanted no part of this reunion. She emailed me, expressing anger and betrayal over this most recent transgression, and told me to "enjoy the family." I was teetering on a precipice, fearing that finding this new branch of my heritage would mean losing her for good. Part of me hoped that I meant too much for her to cast me off again.

My aunt and I took a mini road trip together as she accompanied me to a literary event close to where my birth mother lived. My rental car filled with hours of chatter as my aunt and

I caught up on decades of not knowing each other. In contrast to the crumbs of information that my birth mother had doled out over the decades, my aunt was generous with family stories. I learned that my European-descended birth father was a science professor, that he raised basset hounds and played the trombone. She gifted me with his microscope and a thick bound account of family genealogy, with generations of family trees dripping with ancestors. Their side of the family went back for centuries. I was stunned by this sudden wealth of relatives.

We nibbled our way through my aunt's box of chocolates while we drove. She sat in the front row during the event and applauded wildly after I read. "That's my niece!" she exclaimed, and I teared up. It was an overwhelming gift to be acknowledged publicly after being held in secret for so long. We drove back to her house with my mother's chocolates in my bag. "Those were sure good," my aunt said wistfully. She didn't know the history of these chocolates, what significance they held. "Let's have some more," I said. I unwrapped the white paper of the new box, and we ate them while watching television from her bed. With each empty brown paper cup, I had to admit that my birth mother was gone. Again.

By this time, I was used to her disappearing. I knew I could survive it, just as I had survived her continued secrecy about me—she had waited many years to divulge my existence to her other children. I also knew by now that maybe the door wasn't permanently closed. It still stung, and I was disappointed in myself for holding even a shred of hope for reconciliation.

Four years later, my beloved aunt had passed away and so had my adoptive mother. She and my birth mother had been friendly during the early years of our knowing each other, exchanging holiday cards and occasionally meeting up. For a number of years, my birth mother had sent an annual poinsettia plant to my parents. I emailed my birth mother a link to my adoptive mother's obituary. *Just thought you'd want to know. And by the way, I'm a grandmother now.*

She exclaimed over the photos I sent of her great-grandchild. "Adorable!"

She was back. I allowed myself a modicum of relieved, cautious happiness.

And while I was glad to be back in contact, I felt a foreboding. Now I held my own secret. I had written a memoir about her, about us. And it was going to be published. I had broken the unspoken agreement that I would keep our relationship quiet. But this was my story, something I'd carried, something that had impacted my entire life and identity. I did my best to maintain her anonymity and to portray our relationship with as much compassion, nuance, and complexity as I could. Meanwhile, she sent me chatty emails about her social events, the weather, books she was reading. We were back in a relaxed rhythm. Dreading what I knew would come, I broke the news.

I was saddened but not surprised when, once again, she vanished. I held my breath each time I opened my inbox or my mailbox. But days turned into weeks and months and there was nothing. In publishing this book, I had done the unforgivable. The final estrangement seemed upon us, irreparable.

People congratulated me on the book's success, the awards it garnered. "You must be so happy!" they said. But it was a lot more complicated than that. Finally, I had completed and published my book. I should be celebrating. But I was also mourning. In writing the book, I had broken the yoke of silence. I had, over long painstaking years, crafted a narrative, an identity, and a sense of self. I had found family in my husband, children, and now grandchildren. And once again, it seemed it had cost me the relationship that I'd pursued since I was a young college student. I had made these choices knowingly. Had it been worth it? I wasn't sure. Over these many years, I had longed for a particular kind of relationship with her. I wanted her to be a mother to me. And there were glimpses of this, amid the ambivalence: The time she once brought me soup after I'd totaled my car. The lists of books she recommended to me. Postcards from everywhere. But too often, I wanted more than she was able to give.

I understand that for these long years, my birth mother has been in some form of twilight sleep, numbing her both from pain and the memory of it. Looking back on our decades of intermittent contact, I wonder if our relationship wasn't as readily welcome for her as it was for me because of the trauma it evoked. For me, her presence filled an important, painful gap, while my presence reopened one for her. I finally realized that her disappearances had nothing to do with my worth. It was her own complex and painful history that limited her to this ebb and flow of connection.

Given our many similarities and shared interests, we could have had a deeper mother-daughter relationship. We could have been friends. I would have offered support and care in her later years if she'd accepted it. We could have been the greatest gifts to each other. But it hasn't turned out that way. She has made it abundantly clear that even though she has enjoyed knowing me, off and on, on some level, a familial relationship is not what she wants. Her reticence has forced me to stay in the present moment, whatever small morsel it brings. And even though the lack of certainty is painful, there's a certain bittersweet joy in being surprised.

A little over a year after my book's publication, an email popped into my inbox. "Are you okay?" was all it said. Dumbfounded, I didn't know how to respond. But after I gathered myself, I wrote back, "I'm okay. How are you?" And just like that, our contact resumed.

She signed a recent email, "Wishing you well." It wasn't the "Love" of years past, but like "You are special," it made me happy. I accepted these three words as a small, unexpected gift. I whispered to myself as I walked from room to room. *She wishes me well.* I wish her well too.

Waning Gibbous

Eben E. B. Bein

Seated on the icy toilet
of the getaway house
filled with sleepers, family
chosen, maybe 1 a.m.,
brain gummy with earplugs,
the bathroom door creaks open
—a clench of startlement—

I am in here! I say
too loudly to what turns out to be
no one, just a twitchy latch spring.
I listen, fearing the damage done

but distance is on our side.
No one here sleeps as lightly as you, Mom.

Earlier that day, after running into you
in the grocery store parking lot,
exchanging pleasantries, my friend turned to me and said,
That was okay, right? and then more firmly,
You guys looked okay.

From the bedroom curtain, a beam of silver
escapes. I reach. What we had runs up my arm.

Over the lake—a blind moon
glittering, upturned boats spooning
beneath two trees reaching for each other,
none of their branches touching.

Grips and Pulls

Onita Morgan-Edwards

My eldest son was nine years old when he first pulled his hand from mine as we crossed the Pick 'n Save parking lot. He pulled away a little more when he ran away from home at thirteen, making his way from Venice to Malibu. A little more when someone was murdered on his high school campus. A little more when I preached, "Don't bring no white girl home." *Don't!* A little more when the mother of the white girl he was sneaking around with caught him in the girl's bedroom closet. I got a call that day. "Do you know she is going to Johns Hopkins?" she asked me, running down her personal credentials and the expectation that her white daughter would not see my Black son again. *A veiled threat.* I gripped the phone as her words turned to white noise. *Good!* I thought to myself. *Maybe this will teach him a lesson.* Maybe this would show him the way. Straight. Narrow. Instead, he settled into the life of a chameleon, pulling away a little more. Then poof! Gone.

I was accustomed to dumpster fires by then. Had lit a few, setting myself ablaze. Derailed some relationships and opportunities, sabotaged my own fate, until I learned that playing with fire is dangerous, that crashing into things is painful, and that everyone around me was unwitting collateral damage. Instead of scorching my own house again and again, I learned to shapeshift, code-switch, get by. Crying over my eldest son or spilled milk was a waste of my time. I was by then adept at masquerading my pain with labor: clocking in, chores, church, and other community work, while in my imagination cherubs flapped their wings and sang "Amazing Grace" to me.

I won't say "I'm not perfect!" Hell, you already know.

If I did not pursue him, he would come home, have a relationship with us—that's what I told myself the first five years of his young adult life. Until he didn't. Until he surrendered to drugs and alcohol and made every excuse for why he was never around for his eldest daughter. Until he threatened that I would never see my youngest granddaughter again. He was in his thirties when he finally confronted me about what the problem with *me* was: "We moved a lot." "You let him beat you," he said. "We left California for Ohio." What I heard was: My biological dad was not here, so I never knew him. I heard: I blame you for that, Mom!

While my son had been loosening my grip on him in adolescence, I was preoccupied with two small children, a marriage fraught with rage, addiction, and my husband John's Word of God. I suppressed my needs, walked on eggshells to fulfill everyone else's. My cup was two-thirds empty, and the only things running over were the lies I told myself about making my family work. I coerced myself out of bed and off to work during the week, reminding myself that as much as I hated being a medical secretary, I could at least escape home for a while.

John was violent. He beat all of us. My eldest son would eventually tell me that his stepfather had him pee in cups. Random drug tests were John's nemesis, so he found a way to manipulate them rather than seek the drug treatment he needed. "Did he ever . . ." I asked my son as we stood outside on the back porch. Gritting my teeth and wanting to dig my heels into the concrete. "No," he said. But there were so many other things. So many things my son learned about the world, about his place in it, that crushed his soul. I do not fault him for his responses to these lessons.

John had been dead five years at the time of my son's revelation, one less person for either of us to blame. Still believing that love could fix anything, I insisted that our reconciliation was about nonjudgmental conversations over tea or coffee instead of a 9 a.m. beer. It looked like hugs and tears and pleas for forgiveness. It was, in my mind, letting bygones be gone. It looked like understanding and accountability. Or perhaps it was freedom to be, so long as one's own freedom did not encumber the family's happiness. And so, I set my son free. Free to be whoever he wanted to be. Alcoholic? Okay. Drug addict? Fine. Deadbeat dad? All right. After all, it is his life to live.

As my two other children grew and matured, I'd all but written my eldest son out of our story. I satisfied my urge to blame myself for the chasm between us by chain-smoking and overworking. I rounded myself out by fulfilling the needs of others. I needed to be needed. How else could I feel valuable when I didn't feel valued? Busyness let me hide from confronting my son's pain and my own pain head-on. The longer I performed, the easier it was to deny that anything was wrong. This performance was a superficial shield from his rejection.

After I hadn't seen my son for two years, my body eventually gave in, turning on itself. I spent the next five years in and out of the hospital with a rare blood condition. My blood wasn't coagulating the way it should, and bruises showed up. The bruises did not hurt, but everything else did.

As much as I pretend that I am okay with how things turned out with my firstborn, there's a river of bad blood between us and no justification does this estrangement justice.

Love is powerful, but it cannot save my son from the wiles of destruction that grip him now. I won't apologize for mothering him. Maybe my best was not good enough. I won't say "I'm only human." My compassion for him now is laid bare, made manifest through my commitment to raising his youngest daughter while he remains afield. Through her, he and I remain tethered.

These days, I wear T-shirts emblazoned with *Calvin*, *Karl*, or *Ralph*, bedazzled with little jewels that catch the light just right, in case my son scrolls Facebook. This is my muted rallying cry, a secret, silent wailing. There's still a chance he will see a video of his family dancing and come out from the shadows. Enchanted by his name on my shirts, maybe he will feel the pull of home, each time a little more.

Weird Sister

Nicole Graev Lipson

This story begins, as maybe all do, before the story, with a moment that feels in retrospect like an eerie foretelling. It begins at a New Jersey funeral parlor in 2008, where a group of us had gathered to say goodbye to my grandmother. The mourners included my father and brother Aaron, my uncle Bruce and his family, my grandmother's cousin Bernice—and a bald, stooped stranger in a dark suit lurking just inside the door.

My father's gaze landed and lingered on the stranger.

My god, he said.

The stranger, my dad whispered, was my great-uncle Saul—the one who stopped speaking to our grandmother before we were born. According to family legend, Saul's fury at his sister had to do with a minor detail of my parents' wedding. A guest list oversight? A bad table assignment? When I was a kid, this pettiness astounded me. I did not yet know how family events can be a divining rod for resentment. I did not yet understand the parasitic nature of anger, how it will latch itself onto any small thing it can feed on.

My father greeted Saul, shook his hand, ushered him to a seat. *I can't believe it*, he muttered. *After all these years.*

At the cemetery, I spotted a figure lumbering toward us along the path. Saul. He'd followed us here as well. Afterward, he trailed us to my uncle's house for bagels and whitefish salad. It was as if, after forswearing us for forty years, he was determined to make up for lost time. On the surface, things were pleasant enough. Aaron and I took turns chatting with him and refilling his ginger ale glass, shooting occasional looks at each other—as if to say, *What in the hell?* We laughed a little about the whole thing out of earshot, the oddness of it all. But below my laughter was a dull, thick sadness.

I felt sad because I had lost my last remaining grandparent, the one with whom I was closest. I felt sad because I'd never seen my dad so visibly deflated by grief. But most of all, I felt sad because of this stranger futilely planted on my uncle's couch, who had my grandmother's eyes and cracker crumbs on his lap, waiting like an eager ghost to reconcile with a sister who no longer existed.

My memory of these hours with Saul has become its own haunting, gathering the weight of augury as time goes on. This wouldn't be the case if my brother still spoke to me. But Aaron does not still speak to me—and he has not spoken to me for nearly twelve collective years now.

What did you do wrong? you are no doubt wondering, and I don't blame you, for nothing arouses suspicion like being shunned. I wonder right along with you—though "wonder" is too light a word for my mind's attempts to uncover my transgression. I've spent hours awake in the dark, picking at memories like scabs. I've stared at childhood photo albums until my eyes fatigued, scouring them for clues. I've called my father again and again, drilling him for answers he doesn't have. There's no single moment I can seize onto, no crescendo of shouts or slammed doors as there might have been when I was five and Aaron was eight, when I was nine and Aaron was twelve. I've often wished for such a moment, for the brain craves turning points. My brother's silence is a story with no turning point, a story with no arc. And so it is not a story at all but a living deadness, a low, thumping heartbeat below the floorboards.

I hear the thumping when I'm folding laundry and slicing apples, when I'm watering the plants and walking the dog. It fills my ears each time I climb past the family photos on our staircase wall: my brother at eight, grinning at his paper cone of cotton candy; my brother at twelve, in frayed shorts holding a fishing rod. It is with me at every holiday gathering he does not attend, and on every birthday my children celebrate without him in their life.

Here are the loose plot points I have: Before my brother stopped talking to me, he seemed, for several years, to be dully, ambiently angry. I know that his anger had something to do with our parents' divorce when we were in college, and something to do with the financial fallout of this divorce, and something to do with my forgiveness of our mother, whose affair set in motion the divorce and to whom he also does not speak, the two of us serving time in the same wordless prison. Did he feel abandoned by me when I got married and left New York? (There was that time I worked up the courage to broach how we seemed to be drifting, and he said, *It's not my fault you moved to Boston.*) Could it have something to do with my twentieth high school reunion, when I asked if I could crash on his couch? (His one-word response, *Fine*, felt so laden with subtext that I stayed with a friend instead.) I return to this phone call again and again, poking at it from all sides, because it was after we hung up that my brother stopped calling me and returning my calls. It was after we hung up that a week became a month, and a month became a year, and a year became my children's entire childhood.

One afternoon, when my kids were three, five, and eight, I pulled to a stoplight before the snow-dusted steps of the Museum of Fine Arts. My oldest piped up from the back seat: "Mommy, didn't we go there with Uncle Aaron once?" she said.

"Who's Uncle Aaron?" my youngest said.

Beyond the dusty dashboard, the sky was a leaden apron. What answer could I give my three-year-old when I hardly had an answer for myself? What could I say that wouldn't plant in the minds of these three laughing, shrieking, jostling children, squeezed thigh-to-thigh, a new possibility. That they, too, had the option of erasing one another with silence. That they, too, might one day simply vanish from each other's lives.

"Uncle Aaron," I manage to say, "is my brother."

Blessedly, no one asks any questions—not yet. They think their thoughts, and I think my thoughts, and the car thumps and thumps along the road.

Long before my brother was silence, he was sound. The scrape of a hockey stick on the kitchen floor. The whisper of a ghost story in a backyard tent. The *thwack* of sneakers on asphalt as he taught me to ride a bike. He was music too: a confident pianist, playing Andrew Lloyd Webber hits in the living room; a riotous DJ, blasting songs from the end of the hall. *You gotta listen to this, Nic,* he'd shout, and I'd come running. I listened on his navy rug to the Thompson Twins and Duran Duran; to Van Halen and the Beastie Boys; to Nirvana and the Smashing Pumpkins and REM. I listened with the force of a girl in her big brother's orbit.

At the family dinner table, my brother was a stream of words. He had so much to impart about his day, a near-constant flow of story and opinion and commentary. "You could never get a word in edgewise," my mother said to me recently with a hint of regret, but I don't remember resenting Aaron's spotlight. It simply felt like the natural order of things, him being older and—I can see this now, though I didn't then—him being the boy, with a teeming boy's worth of injury and outrage inside him. Jerome Karetsky had insulted him at recess; his teacher Ms. Grady was singling him out again. His days were a hero's quest and he its protagonist, escaping quicksand, slaying dragons. What were my struggles compared to his? I excelled in school, practiced my pliés in the living room, traded friendship pins at recess. I learned to keep a lid on my small problems, even as they banged and grew inside of me. I made flash cards till my hands cramped and made room for his big feelings. I was never on the wrong side of his problems. Until I was.

This is the story of a brother and sister, but it is also the story of a boy and a girl, a man and a woman. It might also be a story, in its way, of men and women.

At first, I assumed my brother's silence was a phase, a rolling patch of clouds that would eventually pass. Amid the daily urgencies of raising the two small children I'd had by then, it was easy enough to push his absence from my mind. I held tight to our usual rhythms—dialing Aaron's number every few days, holding up my end of the bridge between us. *It's your sister!* I'd chirp when my calls went to voicemail. *Give me a call when you get a chance.*

Then, in October, came my birthday: *Surely, he'll call today,* I thought, but he did not. And then, in January, my oldest's fifth birthday: *Surely, he'll send her a card*, I thought, but nothing came. Each approaching family milestone was now two things at once: a cause for celebration and a looming litmus test that filled me with dread.

The days slipped by.

It's your sister. Hope everything's okay?

It's your sister. I'm here if you want to talk.

Aaron's birthday waited like a fork in my path. I saw, as it approached, that I had two choices: Veer left and return his silence with my own. Keep right and stay the course.

I gathered markers and paper and glitter glue and called my daughter downstairs. We'd always made cards for family birthdays, and his silence wouldn't stop us now. My son poked at blueberries in his high chair. My daughter hummed and scribbled as I slipped my own note in an envelope. That afternoon, at my kitchen table, I'd begun to formulate a personal philosophy of estrangement, one I would come to refine and own with pride. At its heart was a lesson I'd repeated to my daughter often—that while we can't control how others behave, we can always decide how we show up in the world.

And show up for my brother I would, again and again. I'd show up in his voicemail, in his email, in letters to his New York address. I'd show up via our annual holiday card, our youngest's birth announcement, the Evite to my eighties-themed birthday party. I would not allow his version of our story to become my version of our story, or his silence to break the steadiness of my love. I would match his absence with my soft, unshakable presence.

When my brother and I were little, our father often reminded us that no two people were closer in the world than siblings, because no two people share as much of the same blood. "Not even parents and their children share as much DNA," he would say. "There will come a day when Mom and I are gone, but you two will still have each other," he would say. Was he thinking, as he spoke, of his long-lost uncle Saul? Was he trying to keep what churned in Saul's blood from touching us?

The earth turned and a year passed. Another unbelievably followed. The widening gulf between his only children was too much for our father to bear. "I just pray that you two start talking again before my funeral," he said to me during one of his visits.

"Dad, I *do* talk to him," I reminded him. "It is he who does not talk to me." How good it felt to set the record straight. How good it felt to be the calm and virtuous one, safely cloaked in the soothing armor of reason. I did not yet know about the slow-moving poison of silence, how deftly and slyly it works its way under the skin. I did not yet know how it fills the veins with its bitterness until you realize, one day, that you've been slowly, invisibly, changed.

Before my brother was nowhere, he was beside me. His knee by my knee in our backyard tree house, his foot by my foot under the TV room throw blanket. He was beside me in cars and on buses, in oceans and woods, on crosswalks and in elevators and in line at the 7-Eleven for cherry slushies. In our teen years, he was beside me still. The two of us sneaking cigarettes behind the garage and stealing swigs of Smirnoff from our parents' liquor cabinet. The two of us on his moped, my arms around his belly as we screamed down the street spraying gravel.

Before my brother and I were nothing to each other, we were AaronandNicole. *AaronandNicole, you need to clean up your rooms! AaronandNicole, it's time for dinner!* We were AaronandNicole even in our Manhattan young adulthood, among the crew we'd created by merging our college friends. It's so great, his friend Mark said to us, how you two actually like each other. It's so cool, my friend Cat said to us, how you guys are brother and sister but also hang out.

After the drive past the snow-dusted museum, after their shoes have been tossed off and the snack cabinet plundered, my children return to the question of my brother. "Why haven't we seen him in so long?" my oldest asks. "Why don't I know him?" my son asks. As I work to put words to their uncle's absence, I summon my fondest memories to keep my tone light. I construct each sentence carefully, wary of turning them against him should he one day return to us. *Uncle Aaron is a good person but doesn't always manage his feelings well. Uncle Aaron loves us but has a hard time showing it. It's Uncle Aaron's loss, more than anyone's, that he's never gotten to know you.* I stop here before the edge in my voice can grow sharper.

It grows harder every day to keep spinning these forgiving stories, straining to see my brother in the gentlest light. From the far side of his silence, happy memories begin to feel suspect, and other sorts of memories keep surfacing more and more. The time he tricked me into believing the honeysuckles I'd eaten were poisonous and allowed me to believe for an hour that I might die. The time he grabbed my wrist on a long car ride and then forced me to slap my face with my own hand. "Stop hitting yourself," he laughed, for this was hilarious! "Stop hitting yourself," he cackled, while my eyes burned with rage. *Enough, Aaron,* our parents said. *Cut it out, Aaron,* our parents said—the half-hearted refrains of parents who had lost their resolve. This was just their son being a boy again, my brother being a brother again—but I wonder now who the "just" in this common story is meant to protect.

One day, I come across an article in *The New York Times* about the silent treatment. When I read that being shunned by a loved one activates the same regions of the brain as physical pain, I think, *Of course.* Every day now feels like the day my brother tackled me to the TV room rug and knocked the air out of me, and I couldn't get out from under him to say I was hurt.

One evening, when my father calls, his tone has shifted. He's in action mode now, determined for us to put an end to this once and for all. Aaron is a lost cause and will not budge—*I've tried, but he refuses to talk about it,* my father says. His only hope for our reconciliation lies in me. Maybe I could extend some sort of olive branch? A heartfelt letter or an offer to come to New York for a healing talk?

I listen and think, listen and think. I feel my baby girl's cheek pressed against my chest in her carrier, hear the patter of my son's footsteps on the stairs. My neck burns hot as something inside me revolts. *What kind of human forswears his own niece and nephew—and then ignores the arrival of a second niece in the world? What kind of human, given children to love, instead decides to blot out the fact of their lives?* I've been walking the high road for years, but the mother in me can't take a single step farther. I am standing perfectly still but can feel myself slipping, plummeting from my noble hill into a dark abyss.

"Fuck him," I hear myself saying, for it has happened. I've become the villain I swore I'd never be.

I've learned not to mention to people that I have a brother, because the sorts of questions that naturally follow—*Where does he live? Are you two close?*—ignite in me a strange, unpinpointable sheepishness. To convey our story, I must give voice to the story I presume he has made of us, the story where I am culpable and he is blameless, where I'm the enemy and he the aggrieved. Before long, I can inevitably spot it: the shift in the eyes that reveals I'm now a suspect in question. Where there's smoke, there's fire, the saying goes, and perhaps there's truth in this. It's been harder, since I fell to the abyss, to assert my innocence. Sometimes now, when I think of my brother, I'm seized by a wrath that feels dangerously close to wickedness.

I can talk freely about Aaron with my mother, the two of us sharing the sad, wounded bond of the spurned. I can talk freely with my husband—my stalwart defender—whose indignation on my behalf is its own sort of balm. I've slowly learned which friends I can talk with: Lindsay, whose brother stormed out of her house last Thanksgiving; Mira, who hears from her sister only in angry emails; Sara, whose brother fell silent around the same time as mine. We seem to be a bigger club than I imagined, and my late-night internet searches confirm this with data: one recent study suggests that more than a quarter of adult siblings have experienced estrangement. Some researchers believe the phenomenon is a vast, underreported epidemic.

Though I wish my experience on no one, I can't help but feel comforted learning this.

It's comforting, too, to sit on my neighbor Barbara's porch

with a glass of wine one summer night, spilling my secret thoughts into the balmy air. Barbara is a former rabbi who is now a therapist, the sort of person whose presence alone invites true words. It's not the facts that are hard for me to describe, the chain of events, the this-and-then-that. It's not my bewilderment over my offense, or what it's felt like to have, as my only sibling, a living phantom. What's hard to share is my belief there must be some strange, shameful rot at the core of me—for surely no *truly* good person has this happen to them.

Barbara listens, head tilted, her eyes fixed on me behind her glasses.

"There isn't a single strange thing about any of this," she says. "Your story is one of the oldest stories there is."

Under the glow of her porch lantern, she guides me back to Genesis, to the tale of Cain and Abel, where sibling resentment paved the way for the world's first murder. She reminds me of Isaac and Ishmael, estranged forefathers of the Jewish and Arab people, to whom the tensions in the Middle East are often traced to this day. She recounts the story of Jacob and Esau, pitched in battle to win their father's favor; and of Rachel and Leah, opponents in their quest for Jacob's love; and of Joseph and his brothers, who sold him into slavery in a jealous rage.

"Freud thought the great symbol of conflict was Laius and Oedipus, the tension between fathers and sons." Barbara chuckles, like *there goes Freud being an idiot again.* "But over and over, the Torah tells us otherwise. The root of human conflict, it knows, is sibling rivalry."

When I picture my brother, I see him as he looked one of the last times I saw him, in 2013, at a trattoria in Midtown Manhattan, clean-shaven in a crew-neck sweater, his dark hair combed back from his forehead. Things were good. We ate gnocchi. We caught up.

He was forty then, and now he is fifty-two. I do not know how time has worked its forces on him, forming creases around his eyes or peppering his sideburns white. I do not know whether his voice has aged or his posture has changed, whether he's put on a couple of pounds or lost a few.

I do not know Jaime, his partner of the last nine years, though I've heard nice things about her from my dad. I do not know his friends, or what he loves and loathes about his career, or his opinions of our last two presidents. I have no idea what the interior of his new apartment looks like, or what books are on his shelves, or what TV shows he watches, or what disappointments he's weathered or successes he's relished or wisdom he's gained. I no longer know, in many ways, whom it is I have lost.

And he knows nothing of me, of course, a woman with graying roots and deepening brow lines, who can hardly remember what it was to be thirty-six: A former high school English teacher who is now an author, attender of dance recitals and sixth-grade orchestra concerts, runner of a marathon, planner of bar mitzvahs, enforcer of homework hour, reviewer of books, collector of lentil recipes, dreamer of ocean escapes. A tired but hopeful mother in faded sweatpants, trying as hard as she can to create meaning with words.

It seems to me that when you've refused to speak to a loved one for twelve years, that person ceases to be a person. They become a foil character in a formulaic novel of which you are the protagonist. I've come to wonder, as I've puzzled over my brother's distance, if *this*, in fact, might be its ultimate purpose:

to create room for him to mold me, undisturbed, into the fiction of his choosing. How easy it is to make an enemy of those we never see, whose depths and layers and griefs we refuse to witness. When it comes to the silent treatment, silence may be the punishment, but distance and time are its enforcers, ensuring there's no way for empathy or understanding to sneak in—ensuring, as the years compound, that there's no turning back.

I wonder what she looks like, the foe my brother sees when he pictures me, and what form her evil takes. Is she a monster? A criminal? A mastermind? A traitor? Or is she, like so many shunned women, a crone, like Baba Yaga. Or Ursula. Or Hansel's captor. Or one of the witchy Weird Sisters from *Macbeth*, hovering on a foggy heath, speaking words so potent that it makes a man tremble to hear them.

My three children love one another. This is not something I imagine but something I witness every day, as I behold, with my own eyes, what shimmers and flows between them. Through the kitchen window, I see my oldest on the front porch lifting up her sister; on a family hike, I glance up to see my son and my youngest holding hands; passing my son's room, I spot my oldest leaning over him to help with a math problem.

I can hear my children's love with my own ears. I hear it as they call to one another to come and play. I hear it in the funny nicknames they invent for one another. I hear it in the language they share that is not quite mine—the private dialect of the only three people who have grown in the same terrain, nourished by the same water and warmed by the same sunlight and tossed by the same storms.

My children fight, of course—my older two, especially. I cannot stop the glaring and seething, the raging and shouting, from returning to our family's days like a bad refrain. Sometimes when the fights come, I think of Cain and of God's words of warning to him before he murdered his brother: "Surely, if you do right, there is uplift. But if you do not do right, sin crouches at the door. Its urge is toward you. Yet you can be its master."

My brother's silence reminds me daily to stay vigilant, watching, always, for what might be crouching at my children's feet. I now know—from wise mother friends, from trial and error, from parenting articles, from my collection of books on the topic—that there are things I can do to help keep that darkness at bay. I am careful not to compare my children. I avoid pigeonholing them into types. I refrain from arbitrating their conflicts. I try to spread my attention among them evenly. Again and again, I pull my worn copy of the classic *Siblings Without Rivalry* down from the shelf, poring over its pages like a trusted spell book.

And more and more, I try out my own methods of binding my children together. They are the methods of a writer—which is to say, a person who believes in the power of stories to steer how we live. I turn the history of my brother and me into a cautionary tale. I tell them the sad fable of their great-uncle Saul, who learned too late that you cannot love a person who is gone. I narrate for them the Hansel-and-Gretel magic of their closeness, the way they read each other's minds and protect each other. I tell them that once upon a time, they lived, one after another, in the same little house and that this house was my womb. *Only the three of you know what it's like in there*, I say, pointing. My oldest pretends to gag. My youngest roars with laughter. My son tells me, yet again, that I am weird.

And he is right. I am a weird mother, and I am a weird sister squinting into the future as I stir my potions. I say: I can see a day when the three of you will travel together, and live as neighbors together, and grab meals together. I see a day when you will share a Passover table, and hold one another's children, and laugh and laugh at the things you did long ago. When you're troubled, you will call one another, because there's no one in the world who knows you quite the same way. You will fight, and then you will make up, and then you'll fight and make up again. You will find it hard to go more than a week without talking.

I speak as if my words could make it so. I spin for them, over and over, a new kind of prophecy.

Encore for the Boring Daughter

Monique Laban

Act I.

Breakfast and dinner follow the same routine. Don't leave the kitchen table until your parents' story is complete. Listen to them repeat every gruesome detail from last night's true-crime documentary. Nod as they describe yet another dead young woman who was kidnapped, violated, and murdered. Her body found in a ditch. Her body found unclothed. Her body found in several places or never found at all. Wait for them to say what they always say at the end of these retellings.

"It could happen to you."

You're not released from these meals until you respond appropriately. Your eyebrows must shoot up. A gasp must escape your lips. Your parents expect you to express fear. You could become one of these dead young women. You, too, could be kidnapped, violated, and murdered.

Don't tell them what you're actually afraid of. You are scared of being boring like these dead young women. The women of these programs are ordinary. Pale white skin unroughened by pimples. Shiny light-colored hair that doesn't curl like yours.

Women with good grades or stable jobs. Women who liked animals and crafted in their spare time. Women who never did anything wrong. Their deaths are the most thrilling fact about them.

You cannot express boredom, no matter how profoundly you feel it. If you don't give them the performance of terror they crave, your parents scream out all the awful, awful things that could happen to you. Every violent story you've heard them retell since you were seven years old, all rolled into a single, rageful tirade. You will never be released from this kitchen table. You must hear this story, because it is yours.

You're not special, they remind you. You, too, are dull. The only thing that separates you from these women is that you are still, somehow, alive.

Act II.

The first time you attend an opera, your mother insults you.

"Why do you like such weird things?" she asks. She leans forward in the driver's seat as if about to chew off the steering wheel. Your parents are younger than other parents, yet their behavior mimics the seniors in the care facilities where they work. Perpetual grumbling, suspicion at new experiences.

You are sixteen and not allowed to take a permit test, much less drive yourself anywhere. On TV, teenagers in cars are irresponsible, so you are deemed irresponsible. The Philadelphia-based Academy of Vocal Arts, however, is performing an opera at your high school. Your English teacher gave you a free ticket, and because a teacher is attached to your explanation, you can go to school on a Saturday.

You don't even know which opera you're about to see, but you can't spend another weekend at home. Home is where you work the most. Classes don't challenge you, and your after-school job requires only a set number of hours. At home, your parents will always find another chore for you to complete. This weekend, you are exhausted.

Your mother doesn't want your response. Rather, her rhetorical question carries the weight of all the reasons you should feel ashamed of yourself. The price of gas and the fifteen-minute drive. The siblings whom she and your father will have to watch. The cell phone you must borrow from them, since they don't trust you with your own. How she hoped to rest today, but you've pulled her from the TV. None of the dead young women on TV are fans of opera.

You're aware that women die in operas too. Bizet's Carmen gets stabbed by her ex, Don José. Puccini's Tosca jumps off a parapet over the unjust death of her lover Cavaradossi. Strauss's Elektra dies for reasons the audience must interpret for themselves. How could your parents disapprove when these stories end the same way as the ones they love so much?

Act III.

The opera at your high school turns out to be Verdi's *Falstaff*. Unlike your friends' birthday parties that you beg to attend, opera shouldn't seem childish to your parents. What could be more mature than opera? As the wives of Windsor cackle over Falstaff's love letters on a pastel wonderland of a stage, however, your shoes unstick from the auditorium floor. The opera, stranger than you ever imagined, has unanchored you from the world.

And so, you forget your stiff, suffocating clothes that your parents chose so you look like a no-nonsense adult whom they've finished raising, not a teen girl. You forget the silent Japanese family seated next to you and how they purchase ice cream for their children at intermission, an indulgence your parents would never allow. Discomfort and jealousy fall away as Alice's voice soars higher.

Although you give your full attention to the stage, the opera does not intend to immerse you. It doesn't create characters to insert yourself into. Falstaff has no heroic qualities. The drama is so removed from any natural behavior you've seen. Alice and Falstaff roll across the stage in an embrace that's as silly as the prank Alice will pull on him. There are plot holes, poor pacing, and lyrics that you would never speak aloud, much less sing at the top of your lungs. "The lip is the bow / And the kiss is the dart," Fenton and Nanetta say, flirting with each other. The actors celebrate and despair in overexaggerated movements that look nothing like real life, accentuated by the creamy smears of makeup you can spot even from the mezzanine section. The opera puts no effort toward hiding the seams that make it a story.

At all times, you're aware of the boundaries between your narrow Podunk world and the stage's expansive, dreamy one. In this space, your most pent-up emotions are not wrenched out of you, but given room to breathe. Revenge laughs raucously. Fury jeers. Curiosity holds your hand, whispering which alternate endings she would draft. There are stories teeming inside you, ones that you can point to and hold at a distance, and opera has provided a guide for you to follow.

For the next several years, you attend as many operas as your schedule and budget allow. You're welcomed into tissue-thin worlds that you could rip apart but choose not to. You already live in a reality of condescension and meagerness, so why break these rich, nonsensical ones? In dining halls and break rooms, you gush to your peers until their eyes glaze over about

Gianni Schicchi, *Amahl and the Night Visitors*, and *L'enfant et les sortilèges*.

Everyone who loves opera already knows all the tired criticisms leveraged by those who don't. You don't care how many times a line repeats, only that it is sung skillfully. You love the bombast of these lyrics and the singers' larger-than-life command of the stage. Everything you perform for your parents, even your true-crime shock, must be done quietly and politely. No gasps too shrill, no unladylike gagging. Otherwise, they mock you for getting too emotional.

Opera's women may die, but they also seduce bullfighters, trick despots to their dooms, and practice dancing on corpses. They aren't afraid to pursue their passions or leave behind lives that no longer suit them. They are nothing like you, but you desperately want your death, like theirs, to never become the most interesting thing to happen to you. You want a life of stories for yourself. Stories where you do not wait for something to happen; you choose what happens next.

Act IV.

We are the stories we tell ourselves. However, you seem to always play an unwitting role in others' realities, constructed from the narratives with which they surround themselves. To them, it's your fault when you perform in a way that doesn't conform to the worlds they've built. More than anger, it's disappointment that grips you when someone you trusted reveals their limited imagination.

There is the boy-crazy friend with her rom-coms who floods your Facebook page with K-pop stars and implies you're promiscuous for dating outside your race when a white boy asks you to prom. There is the university teaching assistant who consumes so many chosen-one narratives that she spins all your interactions into competitions after you publish in a beloved magazine. There is the murder-obsessed boss who calls you into her office ahead of your first residency, then lists all the stories she knows in which a writer dies. It is easier to villainize you than for them to consider their own lost opportunities. Once you learn how fervently others will choose these fantasies over your harmless victories, you begin to understand why your parents trap you in the same boring story.

Your parents don't stop their retellings even long after you've left home. Over the phone, they prattle on about women like you, pushed onto subway tracks. Women like you, followed into their apartments and stabbed. A global pandemic has frozen the world in terror, yet your parents continue to imagine your life ending in physical violence.

Their most unshakable story is that they never make mistakes. They hadn't been too young to have their first child. They hadn't sped that child up to adulthood out of bitterness. Every measure they've taken toward your upbringing was for your safety, including and especially the spinning of true crime as "cautionary tales."

To preserve their self-image as good parents, they've cast you as the murdered daughter. This character is preferable to a live one who reminds them of how differently they raised each child after her. Driving lessons for your sister, a phone by middle school for your brother, chores that are split evenly among everyone rather than foisted onto you. No one insults anyone's weekend plans. You agree that a dead daughter, silent forever, would absolve them of their faults and validate the reality they've built for themselves. But you refuse to play your role, no matter how many times you've been told what your story is.

Act V.

The only death you can provide is a metaphorical one. You are the high school friend who doesn't stay in touch after graduation. The student who ghosts her former mentor. The assistant who quits her job. The daughter who mails a letter explaining that she will not come home. These disappearances lack the drama or scale that any of these people wanted out of you. Your death isn't entertainment. Instead, your choice to flee them aligns with the spontaneity and stubborn hope you admire most in opera's heroines. Like them, you're sick of confinement, so you wander lively cities, stumble into parties, and toast your friends' successes as they cheer you toward your own.

You've cheated death, in a sense, as you no longer fear living a prescribed life toward a dreadful conclusion. But you must be careful, too. You're not immune to the stories you tell yourself. Halfway through a production of Bach's *Coffee Cantata*, performed in an actual café, you realize you share a dilemma with carefree, unserious Lieschen, whose father prevents her from marrying until she swears off coffee for good. Can she honor the duties the world expects of her while enjoying her guiltiest pleasure? Opera has abetted your escape, but what you take from it most is to never forget reality in favor of any single narrative. Like Lieschen, you're free to choose frivolity or not, and you must ground yourself in the world around you, and these two conditions must always be met. You've freed yourself from the stories that restrict you; the possibilities you've found for yourself will never limit you again.

Each time you find yourself lingering on a narrative for too long—films about runaways, video games about cults, novels about apocalypses—you retreat to the opera, as if resetting yourself. As you take your seat like a tooth lining the theater's mouth, you relax. Here is a story, and no one will trap you inside.

Whiting

Deesha Philyaw

Whiting has been called the "hot dog of the sea" because it's so cheap. But fishermen love this tasty sport fish because it grabs the lure hard and puts up a good fight.

My father said, "Every Sunday morning while your mother lies across town dying, I will make you fried whiting, grits, and cat's head biscuits to make up for telling a judge that you weren't mine. Something to fill your thirty-three-year-old belly for that time I tried to pass you off as my little sister to my new girlfriend, when you were three. A hearty breakfast for those times when you were in grade school and I took you to bars and fed you french fries with ketchup, as you fed quarter after quarter into the pinball machine while I drank bottle after bottle of pink Champale. Some Southern hospitality for asking you to call other women Mama. A home-cooked meal for that time I got you a car but didn't make the payments, so the repo man tracked you down at college and took it back. Something to stick to your ribs for those times when I said I would come pick you up, take you to the fair, give you lunch money, but didn't."

My father said, "I already buttered the grits and the biscuits for you. You know how to pick the bones out the whiting, don't you?"

I do the math, the brittle calculus that this fatherless girl has learned: Take the value of the car my father did not actually buy me, subtract 33 percent rage because the repo man kept his gun holstered. Add five figures in unpaid child support, then carry the time he bragged to me, "I got me a white girl." The answer equals exactly six Sundays' worth of breakfasts, a fraction of what it cost me to gather up the pieces of a girl, shattered like broken seashells gathered from the sands of the ocean floor.

My father said, "This is your inheritance. Spread it like a balm on your broken heart: some fried whiting, some grits, and cat's head biscuits. You know, they call them cat's head biscuits because they are as big around and fluffy as a cat's head."

I did not know that.

For thirty-three years, I put up a good fight. But my mother lies dying across town. Cancer rages and, believing that I must always be looked after in this world, my mother has asked my father to make things right with me. And she has asked me to let him.

She does not, however, give us a blueprint for this.

So come Sunday morning, I eat breakfast at my father's house. I come again and again until my mother dies one August morning. Then I travel a thousand miles back to my other life, the life I left behind to be with my mother as she transitioned while riding upon wave after wave of our laughter spiked with Dilaudid, from this world to the next, after fifty-two short years.

I go back to my life with two wide-eyed daughters and a soon-to-be-ex-husband, a man who is a prized blue marlin of a father.

By December, my father will also be dead. A massive stroke. I don't know this during those six Sunday morning breakfasts. I simply enjoy. I close my eyes and tell myself this is what love tastes like. Every bone in the whiting is an apology. Every grain of the grits, an apology. The cat's head biscuit, a mound of apologies. Everything my father does not say.

Dichotomy of the Rejected

Geneva Phillips

The first estrangement was mandated by the state. There are myriad reasons for this occurrence, stories told and retold from opposing viewpoints. From my side, the effects of a lifetime of untreated trauma, an inability to address the core issues of my dysfunction, coupled with my ineptness at properly executing the meekness and subservience required of me by an uncompassionate and corrupt Children's Services Department. From the side of the state, I imagine, failed urine analyses and a program incompletion, along with my failure to appear at the court hearing where they terminated my parental rights. Things that are, on the surface, incontrovertible. Things which could be explained yet, overall, remain unimportant to the outcome. The die was cast. I received the label "unfit to parent," and my children were remanded to the custody of the state, an institutional and negligent caregiver which I had experienced firsthand, myself, as a juvenile.

Facts can be misleading and in no way represent the shattering. The emptiness. My missing parts. I have struggled over the years to find the exact words that match the desolate landscape

I inhabited in those years, after losing my children to the state. The closest I have ever come was in a poem I once wrote: "The vessel appears intact, it is the inside that is crushed flat."

My children were still young when they were taken from me. I, myself, was in my thirties and had been a mother since I was seventeen years old. But how can one be a mother with no children? How does one unlearn being a mother? How could I survive this unraveling of my identity? I woke each day naked in the shame of my failure. I could never seem to clothe myself against it. Everything that touched me left me raw, exposed, soul-stung. My love was a wound; I could not stop it bleeding. No one told me that grief has no cure. The only way I could endure it was to numb myself to it. Medication and illicit chemicals were my inoculants. I felt trapped by my pain, and I felt I deserved it. The paradox of the toxically bereaved. The tension was unbearable and I sought, ardently, the solace of self-destruction.

Within three years the finality of oblivion was all but within my reach, and during the events of a four-day drug-induced blackout, in an hour-long standoff with the police, after a robbery I committed in broad daylight, I should have obtained it. Yet fate intervened: The police declined to shoot me, despite my insistence, and the knife I stuck in my own throat did not do any major damage. Instead of the surcease of despair I so longed for, I received an eighteen-year prison sentence and an entirely new understanding of misery: my private drowning turned public spectacle.

The second estrangement came during my incarceration. This is harder for me to make sense of, harder to weather, and somehow far more damning than having my rights terminated by the state; at least, that was independent and involuntary of my children's participation. For years I clung to the stubborn hope that once my children had the option to contact me, ostensibly after they were of legal age to make that decision, they would. My heart kept insisting that it was only a matter of time. But my children are adults now, having aged out of the state's juvenile system, and they have opted to remain absent from my life. They have chosen to live their lives unencumbered by a mother.

Being an inmate carries with it an innate sense of shame; already I am perceived as less than human. My willingness to commit an act of blatant criminality sets me apart in a fundamental way from the vast majority of humanity, or so many people believe. I have come to terms with that uncomfortable reality. I have accepted and moved on from the culpability of choices I am responsible for making. However, navigating the shame of being rejected by my own children has been, and continues to be, my greatest challenge to healing. It undermines my wholeness, slapping me at unexpected times. The abnormality of the situation is a constant, unspoken friction that continuously abrades my self-perception with contradictions. Surely, I must be a terrible person if my own children want nothing to do with me. I never know if this is a fact or a question. I vacillate between the two.

"Why" is equivalent to running in circles on a sheet of nails. It is anathema to sanity and emotional stability. Compartmentalization is the only way to weather the severing. Conversations skirt adroitly around the holes in the story. Occasionally my own mother inquires over the phone, "Have you heard anything from the kids?" Her queries grow less frequent with the passing years and her declining memory. It is easier to tell her no, avoiding complex and painful reiterations.

I have gathered second- and thirdhand information about some of my children. This, in itself, is both boon and curse. Always, the conflicting dichotomy of the rejected. I want to know. It hurts to know. For many years I had concocted the self-pacifying belief that my children weren't contacting me because their lives most likely consisted of high levels of adversity and trauma. My own familiarity with post-state custody left me well acquainted with the shambled aftermath such survival entails.

Then I received information that indicated my daughter, at least, was doing well, reportedly living and working in the Oklahoma City area. As happy as I was to know she seemed to be leading a successful life, it dismantled my shield of self-deception. I had to conclude that it wasn't merely circumstance that precluded my children's quest for reunification, but instead, that it was me. I am not someone they have any interest in contacting.

Absence is a confusing thing. Even the body grows confused when a piece of itself goes missing. The abrupt elimination of something vital throws the body into denial, creating phantom sensations to mask the void of insufficiency that confounds the senses, ghost limbs; the body's refusal to accede to an amputation. There is no such remedy for the loss of someone you love. The denial manifests as a series of emotional states. This is no less true for death as it is for estrangement. The cutting feels no less brutal whether by accident or choice. I would like to tell myself I am still a mother, but it is a ghostly impression I cling to, a mask for the void of my insufficiency. There are four children in this world who share my DNA. My name appears on their birth certificates, but of motherhood I have no proof, other than a series of one-sided memories and unreturned affections.

The pragmatist might advise an emotional dissolution to this farcical notion of motherhood after all, what benefit lies in continuing to love and pine for those who are unwilling or unable to forgive or forgo the convoluted narratives proffered by others. I have never been given the opportunity to explain that I am not a monster. I did not willingly abandon my children. However, my children have never bothered to inquire into the veracity of events they may well believe to be true; so the past stands, a distorted banner embroidered by whatever storyteller has claimed their privilege of counsel.

And yet, and yet. I cannot stop loving them, those children I once knew and held so dear. I cannot stop hoping, in spite of all evidence to the contrary, that one day, one day . . . one fine and magical day, my daughter will remember she has a mother who, however imperfectly, loved her. That my sons will remember, in their subconscious minds, the way my hand rested on their heads. How I whispered prayers into their sleeping ears, "You are the best kid in the whole world. You can do anything." And "Momma loves you."

And yet, and yet. This dream has not arrived in fourteen long years. My children are not those I remember; they are grown men and a woman I do not know, existing independently of my scrapbook memory. We are strangers of no moment. A tracery of lives extending from a tangled knot of history, no more in common than what our gene pool suggests. I do not begrudge them their autonomy. I accept and respect their right to live their lives as they choose. I cannot make them love me, but I can give them, and myself, the gift of setting them free: free from my need and unrealized expectations.

That's all any mother can do, really: Just let them go, and wish them well on their journey.

Stranger

Tiffany Aldrich MacBain

I was surprised when my father died, because he'd threatened to live forever. When the hospital called on a bright day in May to say he'd been admitted and was in terminal condition, I delayed my consent to remove the respirator, certain that this latest emergency was another ploy to entangle me in his life. I called my brother, conferred; called back the hospital and spoke with the attending physician, who confirmed that my father's condition was, quote, "incompatible with life."

"You can visit him if you'd like," the doctor told me, "but he probably won't know you're there." As if to clarify, he added, "The lights are on, but no one's home." You remember the things people say to you at times like this, so the image has stuck, my father as a hastily abandoned house, lights ablaze.

My father and I had long been estranged, but lately I'd been drawn back into his orbit, enlisted along with my brother to provide support as our father navigated months of mental and physical health challenges. Over time, the period of his decline began to feel like a march toward death he'd organized to be witnessed by his children. His gait unsteady but insistent, our father made his way toward the end of his life, demanding our attention and our care, and yet, perversely, refusing to accept our help on any terms but his own. It was a destructive year.

From a young age, I understood my father to be different from other dads, and because of him I harbored a general distrust of men. I knew what appearances could hide. Time would eventually ravage him, but in his younger years he was charming and put-together, with hazel eyes and sandy hair neatly cut and parted on the side. He favored starched shirts and navy blazers, steam-pressed slacks, and leather-soled loafers. He liked to look sharp, as he'd say. I suppose this was the man who captured my mother's attention. My parents met in the late 1960s when she was a college student in Sacramento and my father was in town for work. It was a blind date, a setup. It's a wonder that they met, let alone that they fell for each other. My mother was one of seven children, and her Catholic education had conditioned her to stay within the lines—mostly. My father possessed an acerbic wit and a tendency to flout the rules. Maybe she was drawn to that, just as he seemed to like her guilelessness and trust. They were mismatched. Roughly a year after their first date, my mother was living in a fifth-floor walkup on the Upper West Side of Manhattan, married to a man who hadn't bothered to pick her up from the airport when she'd arrived in the city alone, pregnant with me, and no doubt wondering what she'd gotten herself into.

The job in New York was short-lived, and soon after my birth, my parents relocated to New Jersey, where, five years later, my brother entered the world. The marriage was strained from the start, and my parents divorced when I was ten. Many years later, my mom would share that she'd never loved my father, and though it hurt to hear, I couldn't blame her for how she felt. I'd learned to dislike him at an early age. He was arrogant, disconnected, a fearsome specter in our home. He drove sports cars, and always too fast—faster, still, if you said you were scared. I was often scared. He fueled his body with scotch, steak, baked potatoes, and black coffee. I remember the sweet-leaf odor of his cigars, the way he'd chew and spin a tip in his mouth. The clink of ice cubes in a glass still strikes me as menacing, as does the smell of rankly pungent brown booze on the breath of a man. On Sundays post-divorce, my brother and I would spend the day with him. If the fates were on our side, we'd catch a movie. If not, we'd be sequestered in our father's small apartment—a room, really, on the top floor of a depressed house he'd converted into his insurance agency. Football would drone on for hours, my father's attention divided between the game and whatever sci-fi novel he was reading. My brother and I would occupy ourselves by playing with the office equipment. Once, in a desk drawer, I found a stash of *Playboy* and *Penthouse* magazines. The women's poses fascinated and repulsed me, raised mute questions about who I was and what I was for.

All children are vulnerable. The adult heart aches to recognize it, and the usual response is to protect and to guide the young. My father was differently wired. He took pains to humiliate and expose me, and he enjoyed my distress and confusion. I know because he would laugh when he did it, a tight, windy laugh, and his pretty eyes would light up with dark delight. I learned to avoid him, invented a game in which my brother and I would hide behind coats and stay perfectly silent and still so as not to attract the attention of intruders I'd conjured. At night I'd surround my body with stuffed animals, dozens of them, calling each by name as I kissed it good night: Turtle, Lambchop, I've forgotten the rest. Raised Catholic by my mother, I'd pray to God and my guardian angel to bless everyone I knew and, last, me. Before my father moved out, or when I'd have to spend the night at his place, he would sometimes watch me as I pretended to sleep. I'd feel his presence, know intuitively to keep my eyes closed, control my breathing. Surely I had that child's scent about me, of unwashed hair and acrid sweat and something else, sweet and warm. I must have seemed relaxed, and yet I was fully alert, on guard. My father never touched me, but I believe had I opened my eyes he would have taken it as an invitation.

A month before our father died, he received an informal diagnosis of the illness that had defined his adult life: schizoaffective disorder and depression. My brother and I knew in our guts that our dad had other pathologies, too, but we clung to the language the professionals had gifted us. It provided an answer and so came as a relief, even as our father refused to acknowledge or treat the conditions. Throughout our lives my brother and I had endured the judgment or confused sympathy of people who couldn't comprehend our emotional disconnection from our father, let alone the eventual estrangement. But an undiagnosed mental illness—people would understand that. In the 1970s and '80s, when my brother and I were young, there was a limited vocabulary available to describe our father's afflictions. "He's an alcoholic," we would say, and we'd be right, but to me his alcoholism always seemed more of a symptom than a root cause. My mother called him a compulsive liar, and he was that too. Once, he told a roomful of people that I had leukemia. My mother learned about it through concerned phone calls that left her incredulous and embarrassed, and that injected me with shame. My own father had devised and then broadcast the impending death of his child—my death. What else could that mean but that he wished me away?

As I got older, the stories he would tell became more involved and protracted: his (invented) years-long ordeal with lupus, or his (imagined) childhood in County Cork. He began to speak with a terribly formed Irish accent, all lilt and *begorra*. Claimed his real father to have been from the Emerald Isle, claimed his own name to be Sean Michael Gillooly. He said his mother was a prostitute, his stepfather a physically abusive merchant marine. I suspected some of these things to be true—some were, I later learned—but, at the time, there was no telling fact from fiction, no family to ask or ancestry database to consult. Over the years, I've described my father to six separate therapists, choosing my language and examples carefully, yet still they've struggled to comprehend. They've assumed him to be explosive. No. But he was unpredictable, dangerous. Assumed him to be hard. No. He was soft, even gentle, but he was as keen as a blade. Thought he was critical. No, but he was cruel.

He was also intelligent, though he refused to read anything written by women and habitually mispronounced common words. He had a sandy voice that talked over me, interrupted me as if I weren't even there, as if my words didn't matter. If I could have shaken up my father's history and watched the pieces settle into a different order, he might have been a writer or a scholar. Instead, his history and neurology formed him into a man who made a piecemeal career in sales, lived an increasingly isolated existence, and occupied a world of delusion.

My mother was the first to cut ties with him, not when they divorced but much later, when I was in college. For years, she'd worked as the bookkeeper for his insurance agency, partly for income and partly to ensure the alimony and child support payments. During my sophomore year of college, my father was defrauded by his business partner, so he shuttered the agency and declared bankruptcy. He relocated to Los Angeles, where he reinvented himself as a rare coin dealer. With both the money and my father gone, my mother, then only forty years old, found herself free again. She sold our house and moved us to Sacramento—for her, a long-sought homegoing; for my brother and me, a departure. In California, our father maintained his connection to the two of us. We visited him in LA, and one summer my friend and I lived with him while interning in the movie business. That decision proved fateful, for proximity allowed my father to grow more attached to me emotionally, more insistent on my attention and approval. Accustomed to being alternately ignored and diminished by him, I didn't like the change. When my friend left LA at the end of the summer, my father and I were alone together. On the first night, I went to bed as usual, closing the door behind me. Soon enough, I heard him open it and I understood that he was standing on the threshold, watching me sleep. I was twenty-one, but it was as if I were a child again. Almost. As I'd done amid my stuffed animals, I lay still in the guest room bed. I controlled my breathing and willed him to leave. After a time he did, and I lay in the dark and made a plan. Survival for me was no longer play; there'd be no hiding in the closet this time. Instead, I'd protect myself. In the morning I called my supervisor and quit my internship—invented an excuse about needing to get home to help my mom. I packed my things and drove back to Sacramento that day. If my father was going to cling to me, I wanted it to be from across the miles.

A year or two later, he was accused of the fraudulent sale of rare coins. When he abandoned his business and his Malibu apartment, he landed on my doorstep. Though I'd only just graduated, I found him a place to live and got him a job at the sandwich shop I'd worked at in college. When he committed another fraud and the police knocked at his door and arrested him, I was his one phone call.

Well into my thirties, my belief that I needed to rescue my father was tenacious. I knew I felt more exhausted than someone my age should, but I trooped on, issuing my standard refrain, "I'm all he has." Because he asked me to, I drove to the industrial part of a nearby town and retrieved him when he was released on bail. Sometime later, after he'd been sentenced and remanded to jail, I visited the depressed assemblage of cheap hotels and dilapidated shelters in San Francisco's Tenderloin District and, with the help of a friend who spared me the most intrusive questions, packed a small bag of my father's belongings and emptied his room of half-stashed liquor bottles. My father's world was not my own. The place he lived, the people he knew, the things he did were utterly foreign to most of my friends, and I wished they were foreign to me. In the shadowy bedsit, I tried not to breathe in the rank, heavy odor of the air. It stuck to my clothes anyway and clung to my hair. After his release, I continued to take his rambling phone calls, absorb the threats of suicide, dispense legal advice and life advice as if I knew anything about either. Years passed. Eventually he relocated to Seattle's Central District, where he rented a dark basement room with an aged linoleum floor; he slept on a found twin mattress and worked as a telemarketer to make ends meet.

During this time, in the early 2000s, my brother broke ties with our father, less in a single moment of clarity than as the natural outcome of my brother's commitment to his own health. And I, through an accident of the academic job market or fate itself, secured a tenure-line position in Tacoma, Washington, a mere thirty miles from my father's meager room.

Often, without meaning to, we place a burden on our children, perhaps especially our daughters. And so it goes, until someone refuses to play along. My brother had quit the game, and increasingly I yearned to do the same. Within a year of my move, I had a child of my own—a girl—and my world shrank to a single point of focus. Some of this response was biological. When I was a baby, my own mother had similar feelings. I found a note once that she'd written to me when we lived in New York. In it, she described her habit of strolling me around the city, so far from her family of origin and very lonely, but for me. She said that I was her source of joy, that she loved me and was, in a sense, living for me. I felt much the same when my own daughter was born, and perhaps more deeply still due to our situation. My daughter was diagnosed in utero with a medical condition that would require lengthy hospitalization and multiple surgeries. I'd had to schedule the birth in Seattle so as to be near an appropriate NICU. She and I saw each other for the first time through the clear acrylic of an incubator. We locked eyes and I held her tiny hand. I could not pick her up or nurse her; I could not breathe in the scent of her. So I spoke to her and hoped she recognized my voice. And then they took her from me, transported her to another hospital and operated on her. I sent her father and my mother to be with her as I lay alone, bereft and in pain. Through the walls I heard the insistent cries of newborns and the low-pitched, soothing tones of their mothers.

My then-husband and I, new to the Pacific Northwest, had little support. My father lived close enough to catch a bus to the hospital, but the thought of trusting either my daughter or myself to his care was absurd. He had never cared for anyone adequately, including himself; there was no reason to expect he'd be anything but a hindrance now. My husband, a devoted parent, would stay with us on weekends, but work kept him away during the week. For many months, my daughter and I lived mostly alone, together, in a children's hospital. At night, when the place had emptied out, I'd stroll her through the many waiting areas of the hospital complex, show her the fish lit purple in the tanks. For her, I overcame my instinctive fear of the pumps and sensors, learned to reinsert a slipped feeding tube, changed bandages and removed adhesive on her tiny body. This intense experience of caregiving changed me. Circumstance and love had called upon me to be present for my child in ways I hadn't expected to be, and I found within myself a well of strength and a clarity of purpose I didn't know I had.

"I will never look away," I told my daughter one day, a promise I knew I'd keep.

Eventually, my father dropped in on us. He was curious about the baby, but the real reason for his visit was his obsession with his social security benefits.

"I'm worried they'll be frozen," he said, pacing what little space was available in the tiny room.

I pulled back the IV pole lest he trip over it, tested the safety bars on the crib. I leaned wearily over my daughter, concerned that my father's agitation would upset her. She slept.

"I'm sure it will be fine," I said. "You served your sentence."

"I broke parole," he insisted. "I left California. There could be a bench warrant out for my arrest."

I suspected that the California penal system had bigger problems than my father, but I suggested he call to check on his status. He didn't want to tip off the police. I asked if he'd contacted the social security office. Likewise, he said, he feared drawing their attention to the problem. Back and forth we went, him talking in circles, and me running low on ideas and patience.

"Dad, I can't deal with this right now," I said at last, an edge to my voice.

He ignored me.

I have a vivid memory: he and I standing on either side of my daughter's hospital crib, her tiny form, wired and tubed, between us. Anyone gazing upon such a scene would have pitied her and me, I think, and marveled at our fortitude. But my father looked beyond her, looked through me. He saw only himself, and he talked on.

This is not love, I thought. *You do not love me.*

Two years later, my father interrupted our first family pumpkin carving with an emergency phone call. I dropped the knife, left the guts on the floor for my husband to clean up. In the car on the way to my father's apartment, my heart raced and my temples throbbed. I pulled over and called my brother.

"I have to take Dad to the ER," I said, hyperventilating. I thought maybe I would die in that dark blue Ford Focus, idling at the curb of a residential street. "He's in pain. He can't see."

"You don't have to go."

My brother's words, calmly delivered, shocked me into clarity.

"What do you mean? Of course I have to go." My logic was implicit: *I'm all he has.* The year before, in spite of my refusal to allow my father to move to Tacoma, he had done just that. He'd been wrong about the social security problem and now drew just enough each month to afford a rent-controlled senior apartment in my town.

"Listen to me," my brother said, his voice soft, even. "I mean it. You don't have to go." This was the therapy talking, and the quiet resolve he'd cultivated over years of setting boundaries.

"What will he do?" I asked. "He can't afford an ambulance."

"You can call him a cab."

I felt my heartbeat, focused on my breath. In the stillness, I accepted the plain truth of my brother's words. I arranged for a taxi. I then called my father, who refused to accept the new plan. Though effectively blind from what we would come to learn was sepsis, he returned to his apartment from the sidewalk where he'd been waiting for me outside in the cool dark of autumn. Eventually, I was to learn, my father called an ambulance.

For the next day or two, I attended to my routine: prepping and teaching my classes, caring for my daughter, spending time with my husband. I felt no guilt over the decision I'd made because I'd made it from a place of clarity. At long last, I'd set the terms of our engagement. My father might not like the change, but he had no choice but to accept it.

I did visit him in the hospital. An employee intercepted me on the way to his room to stress the need to find a rehab facility. My father was a difficult patient and had few resources and no private insurance. Hospitals don't tend to want people like him. Hastily, tensely, we made arrangements.

In the dark of his room, my father recognized my voice. He stared at me with sightless eyes and implored me to get him out of there.

"They're harvesting organs," he said, terror in his tone. "They come at night and put you on a boat. Then they cut into you and toss your body over the side."

He made a full recovery because, to the detriment of my own mental health and my first marriage, I saw him through the ordeal: visited him in the rehabilitative care facility; cleaned his apartment, did his laundry, and stocked his kitchen. I helped, too, with his transition back home and ushered him to follow-up appointments. His clean bill of health signaled the end for me. My father had lived to see another day, but I was no longer interested in being his helpmeet. As we sat side by side in the waiting room of an optometrist's office, I told him what I needed to say.

"That's ridiculous, Tiffany," he said, turning to look at me. He wore an expression of amused surprise. "Of course I love you."

"No," I said simply. There was no heat to my words, only candor. "You don't. And anyway, it doesn't matter. I need a break from you."

My father shifted in his seat. "That's fine," he said, as if the request struck him as reasonable. "How long?"

"Longer than a few weeks," I said. "I'll let you know when I've had enough time."

I remained estranged from my father for the next ten years. He'd send cards to my daughter for Christmas, and I'd quietly tuck the five- or ten-dollar bill in her piggy bank, tossing the card signed *Gramps.* My brother and I had needed protection from our father when we were children, and while the divorce offered us some separation and shelter, it was not enough. He did harm, our father, and I would shield my daughter from the danger that he posed.

Sometimes, as I drove her to her elementary school, I'd see him walking, no doubt to catch a bus or buy a few groceries. I wouldn't point him out to her; I'd simply absorb the momentary shock and file away the visual proof that he was clean and upright. Once at a grocery store, we collided with each other as we rounded an aisle from opposite directions. I knew instantly that it was him, but his attention was elsewhere. He didn't look up as he said "Excuse me," and I didn't touch his arm and say "Dad." Occasionally, my brother or I would receive a handwritten letter that indicated our father's paranoia and delusion had intensified. When he wrote to request assistance in hiring a television attorney to defend him against imagined adversaries, we involved Adult Protective Services. Though I no longer had a relationship with my father, I lived with the knowledge that one day a call would come, and everything would change.

It happened in the fall. In my office on a Saturday, I took a deep breath and returned the call of the social worker who'd left the message. When we spoke, she sounded uneasy, tentative. I recognized the tone. Like many people before her, she couldn't piece together the disparate facts of my father's existence: Her patient's daughter was a local professor, well spoken, even responsible. And yet, she told me, her patient had been admitted for adult starvation and failure to thrive. The situation struck her as, well, strange. In spite of myself, I was also confused.

Starvation? Failure to thrive? I stood over my desk in the dim afternoon light, the phone receiver pressed against my chest, and I thought, *Just like a baby.* I thought, *Maybe now he can be in my life.*

A few hours later, my father interrupted my dinner out with my second husband and a friend who was in town for a conference. I stepped outside to take the call, and for the first time in ten years I heard his voice. It was older, tired, a piece of scrap worn thin with worry. When I was young he used to say, when my brother or I would pick up the phone, "Hello, this is your biological father." He thought it was funny, an ironic nod to his lack of interest in being a parent. I fancied then that it also masked his pain. While he'd continued to loom large in our lives even after my parents' divorce, he was the outsider, the outcast. He was alone.

This time he said, "Hello, T. It's Dad."

Outside of the restaurant, an ember of duty or hope kept me on the line. I told him I'd visit him the next day. I told him everything would be okay.

In the hospital, my father was small, diminished. A white-and-blue gown hung loosely over his bony form; he was naked underneath. I know because he moved carelessly when he tried to get out of bed, the gown gaping and revealing more of him than I cared to see. He wanted to give me his keys, send me to his apartment for his checkbook and some spending money, which he thought he'd need to tip the nursing staff. I agreed to go. I wanted to find him some clothes to wear, and I wanted to understand how a person with a checking account and cash goes hungry.

I should have known better, should have prepared myself to reenter my father's realm. I'd been to his spaces before, sensed the insanity that gestated there. When I entered this one, I noticed the lights had been left on. Directly before me, on the worn shag carpet of the living room, were towels and electrode patches, discarded by EMTs in the course of rescuing my dad. Directly behind, leaning quixotically in a corner, a fencing sword, tip down. On a shelf, a small ceramic container, corked and empty and bearing the legend, "Your inheritance." My father seemed to have made his couch into a bed. I moved aside the pillow and a pale blue sheet and felt between the torn and sutured cushions, as he'd instructed me to. I pulled out an envelope, stuffed with nearly five thousand dollars in cash.

Adjacent to the living room was a small kitchen, with mustard yellow floors and cabinets of chocolate brown. Here, though my father had been starving, I found food—so much food. A pan of succotash, heated on the stovetop and then left to grow mold. In the freezer, pork, sausage, corn, peas. More food in the refrigerator; in the cupboards, more food still. My father had gone shopping, unpacked grocery bags, prepared a meal, and then he had refused to eat it. I saw stacked mail and assorted papers on top of the microwave, discovered cramped handwritten notes that detailed the movements of CIA operatives on the roof of his building and in his walls, notes that traced his food from the nearby Safeway back to a poisoned river in Southeast Asia. I stood amid the organized chaos and let the facts fall into place.

The apartment visits became a hated ritual. Upon each hospitalization, I'd retrieve a green duffel bag containing his financial history, meager personal items, and the envelope of money from his place. Each time I entered I noticed changes to his home, signs that his illness had intensified and his grip on reality, already tenuous, had loosened. Toward the end, I found feces fused to the carpet and dried vomit in the bathroom. After each visit, I would return to my own home, strip down in front of my washing machine, stuff my clothes inside, and walk upstairs to the shower, a cleansing one part physical and two parts psychological. My brother and I resigned ourselves to phone calls from him, from first responders, from social workers and care managers. We became voices of reason expert in explaining our father's history.

"He doesn't have a gun," I reassured a rattled medic. "Only a sword."

Those days assumed a bleak predictability that screened the reality that our father was inching us toward a conclusion foregone since my brother and I were children and well before that. He was dying. He wanted us to save him, and he wanted to go.

Long before his death I had processed this loss, learned to live without him. The practice of estrangement has been around for centuries, a painful history captured in definitions now obsolete but still resonant: I severed my father from my community, removed him from his dominion, for he had become remote, beside himself, maddened. The last time we spoke was about a month before his death. He was at the end of an involuntary commitment for psychiatric care secured in part by my testimony. While institutionalized, he had been evicted from his apartment and his belongings removed—the cash had vanished—and now he faced two options: be released to homelessness or be transferred to the long-term care facility my brother and I had arranged for him. We urged him to move into the facility.

"If you've ever loved me," I said, "please, Dad. Do this for me." Knowing that my father was physically safe—that he had a place to live and money enough to survive—had allowed me some peace of mind during our estrangement. As he faced the next phase of his life, I was desperate to be spared the agony that would come of his making the wrong decision. Desperate, too, to believe what he'd said years before to be true: *Don't be ridiculous, Tiffany. Of course I love you.*

He listened to my plea and then chose to go it alone.

"How will you survive?" I asked.

"I'll live by my wits," he said.

I would see my father twice more, once as he lay sunken and gray but alive in a white bed, and once as he lay there dead. The final hours of his life were the more difficult for me, because although I had been warned that my father would not be conscious, I saw that my permission to remove the respirator had made his every breath a labor; he did not seem at peace. Dying looked hard, so I spoke to him sparingly, softly. I imagined it was possible that within his brain weak synapses dimly fired at the sound of my voice, my words rejoining two ends of a severed tie.

"I'm here," I said. "I came back."

Perhaps now he could rest more easily. Perhaps so, too, could I.

"It's okay to go now."

The next day, his body was still, its work was done. The nurses had cleaned my father and changed his sheets, made him nice for my brother and me. I sat alone next to my dad for a few minutes. I was slow to absorb this new reality. I touched his chest through the thin blanket, felt his solidity. I uncovered his left hand, took it in my right. I could not remember having held my father's hand before, but I knew it by heart. How strangely familiar he was to me.

And Still

Jane Wong

An arranged marriage made me. Strangers standing
to pose for a wedding photo made me. Hands folded like
envelopes or touch-me-nots. Cigarette smoke and lily pond

pucker. Across so much ocean, a stew of fish flashing back
a heart or two. Okay, I'm making this up. There is no photo.
What I've been thinking about lately: I haven't seen my father

in so many years, I worry I might not recognize him. That's not
true. I could pick his mahjong eyes rustling regret from any
lineup. I hope he is well, hope he makes scrambled eggs in

the morning, fluffy as a down comforter. That he is drinking
less, even one tiny gemstone less. Hope he still remembers
the blizzard of '96—such hurtling heaps of oceanic snow—

and wonders if I ever did wipe the ambered snot from my nose
then or was he supposed to help with that? Maybe he is looking
at his sleeves now, considering their kid snot-wiping capacity.

I have so many white hairs coming in, underneath like a vast
crinoline. And still, I've been thinking these things.

He Blew It

Stephanie Foo

Before I officially cut contact, my father started calling me frequently, sometimes once a week, sometimes multiple times a day. He lived in California, I was in New York, a twenty-eight-year-old working in a high-pressure newsroom. I begged him to schedule calls with me, to please text first, to call me after work, but he never did. He'd call me during my workday, and even if I was in a meeting, I'd excuse myself to pick up. I picked up because I felt he needed me. I picked up because I was scared of what would happen if I let him go to voicemail.

In these conversations, he told me he was depressed. Lonely. My stepbrothers had become distant, recalcitrant teenagers who didn't need him anymore, who just wanted to play video games. He said they weren't even his real kids, that I was his only *real* child. "Maybe," he mused, "I should leave them, just start over."

For years, I'd dreamed of him saying these words to me. When I was thirteen, my physically and verbally abusive mother abandoned our family. It was a very tough time. My father took her departure perhaps harder than I did—he was devastated by her rejection and often talked about killing himself, whereas I was mostly grateful to not be severely beaten every day. I became his caretaker, his de facto therapist, his comfort, and his best friend. It was a daunting role for a teenager, but at least we were closer than ever. For my entire freshman year, we were two peas in a pod, sharing music, going to shows—I picked out a new wardrobe for him, consisting mostly of Hawaiian shirts. However, in my sophomore year, my father started dating other women and staying out for days at a time. By my senior year, he'd found a girlfriend with two very young boys and moved in with their family, deserting me. He left me the house, in which I lived completely alone. We rarely spoke, though sometimes when I came home from school, I'd find a rotisserie chicken on the counter.

I resented the children who had stolen my father. Not just stolen, but reformed. He had been distant in my childhood, preoccupied with work and golf, but he had become a stay-at-home father to these boys. Even at our closest, he'd never attended my school tennis matches, but he went to each of their sporting events. He'd only fed me at restaurants when I was a teenager, but for them, he learned to cook my favorite dishes—lotus root soup and steamed eggs and babi kecap. He changed diapers and cooed at his shiny new family while I shoplifted hot dogs to survive and cried myself to sleep in an empty house, wondering, *Why had he chosen them over me? How did they inspire such love?* I had fought bitterly with him. I'd been raised by my rageful mother, after all, so I was a traumatized coil of barbed wire, quick to curse and spit. *Did I remind him too much of her? Were they gentle and easy by comparison? Why wasn't I enough for him to stay?*

After he left, our relationship became strained. I was angry and volatile; my father was dishonest and avoidant. He didn't come to my graduation or drive me to my new dorm when I left for college; instead, two months after I left, he secretly sold the house I'd lived in and threw out all my belongings without my consent. Sometimes he tried to buy my love with dinners out, a digital camera, handles of Popov vodka. But we'd easily go six months without speaking. Especially after I moved to New York for work, I rarely heard from him, and he did not visit.

But with these new phone calls in my late twenties, he reappeared. I was needed once again. Not just by him, but by my stepbrothers. Along with his threats of leaving his new family, he was again expressing suicidal thoughts. Though I'd still never even met my stepbrothers, I now felt protective. The grief of losing a parent as a teenager—I wouldn't wish that on any child. Even a child I'd spent years of my life hating.

"You're being ridiculous," I told him. It was perfectly normal, even healthy, for teenagers to be avoidant and moody. They'd level out eventually. He hadn't been able to wait that out for me, and see where it had landed him? "You have a second chance at this parenting thing," I urged. "Do. Not. Blow it."

For months, I counseled him, sometimes multiple times a day. He took my advice. Instead of harboring passive-aggressive resentments at his wife, he started asking her about her feelings and learning about her menopausal hormone changes, her annoying boss. He understood that her flashes of anger weren't directed at him, and he didn't need to take them personally. He tried to connect with his sons in the evenings and had long discussions with them. He told me that he was beginning to understand his family on a deeper level. At my urging, he even started going to therapy. He thanked me eagerly. And when his relationships improved, he stopped calling.

That's not entirely true. Sometimes I'd see his name on my phone at work, and, ever-loyal, I'd pick up. They were all butt dials. "Hello!" I'd shout. "I'm in your pocket! Hello!" He didn't hear me. Often, I could hear him talking with his sons.

A few months later, I was diagnosed with complex PTSD. This revelation transformed the way I saw myself and the world. I realized how profoundly my childhood trauma influenced my day-to-day life. The constant mysterious bruises I had all over my body from crashing into stuff—thanks, intense dissociation! My hypercompetitiveness and perfectionistic, workaholic tendencies—surprise, getting horrifically beaten every time you get a B+ has consequences! My troubles with men and the way my friendships often blew up—oops, turns out if you weren't given unconditional love as a child, you can become an insecure weirdo with a major abandonment complex! The depth of my hurt seemed boundless, so I turned my rage to the origins of it. My parents had done this. My father had broken me. And now, what was he doing to pay me back? To help *me* heal? Perhaps love wasn't love if it only took and never gave. Perhaps, through that lens, he'd never loved me at all. So I emailed him and told him: We were done.

I knew, logically, that I'd made the right choices in my estrangement. But cutting contact still hurt. A nasty little voice in my head remained, whispering, "Oh, come on now. The abuse wasn't that bad. Maybe you're just not appreciative enough. Not willing to work hard enough. Not patient enough, forgiving enough, empathetic, brave enough. Not enough."

I went to a lot of therapy. Years passed. I got married. I wrote a book about healing from complex PTSD, *What My Bones Know*, and published it. The voices eventually grew quieter. And then I heard the news.

He blew it. After all that, he blew it.

He'd cheated on his wife and abandoned his family for yet another one. I heard the news from my now-former stepbrother, via Facebook messenger. He told me that my father had cut contact with him and his brother, the two boys he'd lovingly raised from toddlerhood. "Since he's distancing himself from us, I hope he can find some peace," he said. "If he's ready to talk, I will listen." A truly generous, kind approach. More generous than I was willing to be.

My first reaction was guilt: If I'd kept in contact and continued counseling him, could I have gotten him to stay? Could I have healed his family? For my former stepmother, I felt pity but also a little petty. *You lose them how you get them.* Mostly, I felt a deep sadness for my stepbrothers, whose pain I knew far too well. I prayed that they would fare better than I. That they wouldn't let this abandonment damage their self-worth, their belief in their intrinsic value and lovability. I offered my support, but they never took me up on it. Fair—we'd only spoken once or twice during my father's whole marriage, and the only thing we now had in common was a void.

I have to admit, though, that after the shock subsided, my tumultuous feelings settled into relief. A full-body release of something I had not known I was holding.

It wasn't *me* he had abandoned. Not me personally, not because I was too inconsistent, too needy or angry. I was simply another victim of his own hurt. This was a man who was plagued with a loneliness so deep, he wasn't able to self-soothe through tough relational periods. Instead, he ran from conflict, even from conflict with his own children. This was a man who hadn't done the work of healing and never would.

One of the unfortunate symptoms of surviving complex trauma is the belief that every conflict or loss is your fault. It's a safety mechanism—if it's your fault, then it's within your control. You can prevent that next slap or insult, if only you can be perfect enough.

But the reality is that most of us can control very little about other people. We cannot determine how they act toward us, what they think of us. You can't fix anyone who doesn't want to be fixed. You can't do someone else's emotional work for them. And you can't make anyone love you, not even your own parent, no matter how much you work, give, cajole, and therapize.

That's terrifying. As a survivor, I hate helplessness. I love control. But surrendering control is an exhilarating freedom.

Because if I could never have been perfect enough for my father to stay, to love me—then it's okay that I am imperfect. It's okay that I'm human, that I have legitimate needs and desires. Other people, the right people, love me in all of my complicated beauty. My two dear friends I met in the fourth grade, for example, forgive me even when I am annoying, hot-tempered, and anxious, and when I am sad, they buy me expensive sushi and give me hugs. My husband and I fight all the time, but we both work equally hard to make solid repairs, and he laughs at my grumpiness, my flatulence, my inability to do simple math problems. My chosen family loves me not in spite of, but *because* of my flaws. They teach me what I deserve—whole, uncompromising, reciprocal love. Now, when I don't receive that, I find it easier to say, "It's too bad I wasn't to your taste. But that doesn't mean I need to change."

That little voice that nagged me in the middle of the night, that demanded whether I should have been braver, gentler, more giving—I don't hear from it anymore. Not since I looked it in the face and said, simply, "I am enough."

The Empty Bowl

Cheryl Strayed

Author's note: Years ago, a conflicted young woman wrote to my Dear Sugar advice column, asking whether she was right to sever the relationship with her abusive father. The excerpt below is adapted from my response.

Our parents are the primal source. We make our own lives, but our origin stories are theirs. They go back with us to the beginning of time. There is absolutely no way around them, even if they're dead or long estranged from us, as my parents are. My mom died when I was twenty-two and my abusive father essentially left my life when I was six.

I've lived so long without them and yet I carry them with me every day. They're like two empty bowls I've had to fill on my own again and again.

After my mother died, I wrote a letter to my dad. I hated him by then, but there was a bright crack in my hate that had been made entirely by my mother's love, into which my father could have slipped if he'd changed. In the letter, I told him my mother had suddenly died and also that I had always hoped that someday we could have a relationship. I said that in order for me to do that, he first had to explain to me why he'd done the things he'd done when we'd been together.

Sometimes I imagine my father opening that letter. It was twenty years ago and though just about everything in my life has changed in those twenty years, my imagining of my father receiving the letter with news of my mother's death has not. In my mind, he cries softly at the news. He realizes his three children are now orphans and here's his chance to make things right. Here's his chance to be our dad. It's not too late. We need him now.

But he didn't realize that. Instead, he got drunk and called to say that I was a lying bitch and that our mother had tainted our minds and turned my siblings and me against him. I hung up without saying goodbye.

Seventeen years passed.

Then one day the phone rang and there it was: my father's name on the tiny screen of my telephone. *He's dead*, was my first thought. I believed his third wife was calling to tell me that. I didn't pick up the phone. I only watched it ring. I listened to the message a few minutes later.

It wasn't my father's third wife. It was my father. "This is your father," he said, followed by his first and last name, in case I didn't know who my father was. He told me his phone number and asked me to call him.

It took me a week to do it. I was done with him. I had filled up the empty bowl of him over and over again. I had walked barefoot across a bunch of crap carrying it in my hands. I hadn't let anything slosh out. I didn't love him anymore. I only remembered that I had loved him. So long ago.

I dialed his number. "Hello," he said—his voice so familiar after all this time.

"This is your daughter," I said, followed by my first and last name, in case he didn't know who his daughter was.

"Do you watch Rachael Ray?" he asked.

"Rachael Ray?" I whispered, barely able to speak, my heart racing.

"Rachael Ray, you know. The cookbook writer. She has a talk show."

"Oh, yeah," I said.

And on it went, the most flabbergasting conversation I've ever had. My father spoke to me as if we spoke every week, as if nothing that had happened had happened, as if my whole childhood did not exist. We chatted about low-fat recipes and poodles, cataracts and the importance of sunscreen. I got off the phone fifteen minutes later, utterly bewildered. He wasn't delusional or ill or giving into age-induced dementia. He was my father. The man he'd always been. And he was talking to me as if I was his daughter. As if he had a right.

But he didn't. Shortly afterwards he sent me a chatty note over email. When I replied, I said what I'd said in the letter I'd written to him years before—that I would consider having a relationship with him only after we spoke honestly about our shared past. He replied inquiring what it was I "wanted to know."

I had come so far by then. I had accepted the facts of my life. I was happy. I had two children and a partner I loved. I wasn't angry with my father anymore. I didn't want to hurt him. But I couldn't pretend to have a relationship with him if he refused to acknowledge our life. I was prepared to listen. I wanted his insight, to know what he thought, and also to see if by some wondrous turn of events, he'd become a different man—one who could at last be my dad.

I wrote the most generous, loving, true, fearless, painful, mature, and forgiving letter I could muster. Then I pasted it into an email and pressed send.

My father's reply came so quickly it seemed impossible that he'd read the whole thing. In enraged words he wrote that I should never contact him again and that he was glad to be finally rid of me.

I didn't cry. I laced on my running shoes and went out my front door and walked through my neighborhood to a park and up a big hill. I didn't stop walking until I got all the way to the top and then I sat down on a bench that looked over the city. It was the week before my thirty-ninth birthday. I always think of my parents on my birthday, don't you? And I imagine it in the same way I imagine my father getting the letter I wrote to him after my mother died—it doesn't change, no matter what happened afterwards. I can conjure my mother and my father so clearly on the day I was born. How truly they must have loved me. How they must have held me in their arms and thought that I was a miracle. They must have believed they could be better people than they'd been before. They would be. They knew they would. They had to be. Because now there was me.

So it felt particularly acute to sit on that bench absorbing what had just transpired. I had that feeling you get—there is no word for this feeling—when you are simultaneously happy and sad and angry and grateful and accepting and appalled and every other possible emotion, all smashed together and amplified. Why is there no word for this feeling?

Perhaps because the word is "healing" and we don't want to believe that. We want to believe healing is purer and more perfect, like a baby on its birthday. Like we're holding it in our hands. Like we'll be better people than we've been before. Like we have to be.

It is on that feeling that I have survived. When you reach the place that you recognize entirely that you will thrive not in spite of your losses and sorrows, but because of them. That you would not have chosen the things that happened in your life, but you are grateful for them. That you have the two empty bowls eternally in your hands, but you also have the capacity to fill them.

That's what I did the day before I turned thirty-nine. I filled the empty bowl of my father one last time. I sat for so long on that bench looking at the sky and the land and the trees and the buildings and the streets, thinking: My father—*my father!*—he is finally, finally, finally rid of me.

Acknowledgments

No Contact would not exist without the writers whose words grace its pages. My heart bursts with pride at the community assembled in this book. Incredible writers, yes, but also wonderful humans. What a privilege and joy to have gotten to know each of them through the editing process! I am forever grateful to these thirty-two souls for putting their faith in me and my vision for this collection.

Over the past few years, hundreds of writers reached out to me with essays, pitches, and heartfelt messages. Thank you. I wish I could have stretched the pages of this book to include you all.

This project struck a chord right away. How lucky for me that it landed in the hearts of Martha Wydysh, the kindest, fiercest agent I could ever wish to have on my side, and Alicia Kroell, a brilliant editor whose intelligence and compassion made our collaboration on this tough topic a delight.

On my list of ideal publishers for *No Contact*, Catapult was at the top. What a gift to be granted this wish. Thank you to Kendall Storey and Alyson Forbes for their steadfast support of this anthology, and to Rob Shapiro for jumping in with such care and warmth. Many thanks also go to Laura Berry for her diligent wrangling of all moving parts and her beautiful layout; to Nicole Caputo for hitting the bull's eye with that gorgeous cover design; to Wah-Ming Chang and Olenka Burgess for their production expertise; to Marinda Valenti for her eagle-eyed copyedits; to Rachel Fershleiser, Ashley Kiedrowski, and Lily Philpott for their marketing savvy and enthusiasm; and to my publicity buddy Megan Fishmann for being a marvel to work with.

Special thanks to Anna Brones, a Pacific Northwest artist

whose papercut wonders have a special place in my heart and on my walls, for the use of her stunning "Solitude"; and to Julia Maziarz and the Business Affairs team at Trident Media Group for their help and moxie.

For their kindness and wonderful blurbs, thank you to Ocean Vuong, Mira Ptacin, Sonora Jha, Harriet Brown, Jessica Berger Gross, Minda Honey, and Kelly McMasters.

I am part of a fantastic literary community whose support buoyed me through this project: Margot Kahn and again Kelly McMasters, without whose guidance and generosity this anthology might never have come to life; my Tuesday writing cohort, Dhana Musil, Siobhan Ring, Cynthia Welte, Joann Peterson, and Megumi Ito; my beloved memoir discussion group, Alyson Shelton, Ronit Plank, Devon Fredericksen, Nicole Graev Lipson, Aimee Seiff Christian, and Natalie Serber; my lit mag pals, Cindy DiTiberio and Brianna Avenia-Tapper; and so many writing and editing friends near and far, in particular Mary Boone, Laurie Frankel, and Naomi Eagleson. Thank you all.

For their invaluable friendship through the making of this book and beyond, I am grateful to MaryAnn Viviano, Tiffany MacBain, Cassie Lewis, Elisa Ford, Eric Ford, Nicole Siciliano, Jessica Bjorklund, Michele Shepherd, David Savage, and Krista Johnson.

I am fortunate to be loved by my mother and to have lucked out in the step- and in-law department. Much love to this motley parental crew for being steady and true.

A final word of gratitude, to my husband and children: I love you beyond what words can express. Thank you for showing me the meaning of family.

About the Contributors

Hannah Bae is a freelance journalist and nonfiction writer who is at work on a memoir about healing from childhood trauma and family estrangement. In 2024, she was a New York State Council on the Arts grantee in literature and a nonfiction juror for the Kirkus Prize. Bae was the 2020 nonfiction winner of the Rona Jaffe Foundation Writers' Award, a 2022 and 2021 Peter Taylor Fellow for the Kenyon Review Writers Workshop and a 2019 fellow at Asian American Writers' Workshop. Follow her on Instagram at @hannahbae.

Eben E. B. Bein is a biology teacher turned climate justice educator, intergenerational organizer, and multidisciplinary artist. They were a 2022 fellow for the Writing By Writers workshop and winner of the 2022 Writers Rising Up "Winter in Variations" poetry contest. Their words can be found in the likes of *The Atlantic*, *NOVA* (PBS), *PINCH*, *Nimrod*, *New Ohio Review*, and four anthologies. Their first chapbook, *Character Flaws*, won *Fauxmoir*'s Spring 2023 chapbook competition and meditates on judgment in intimate relationships. They are currently working on their first full-length collection about parent-child conflict, healing, and love. They live on Pawtucket land (Arlington, Massachusetts) in a house they co-bought with their husband and poet friends.

Soni Brown is a Jamaican-born, Colorado-based writer for a university and a comic-memoir educator. She holds an MFA in writing and earned fellowships from Tin House, PREE Writing Studio, and Mendocino Coast Writers' Conference. Her work appeared in *Cosmopolitan*, *The Believer*, *Desert Companion*, *Sisters from AARP*, *New York Daily News*, *F(r)iction*, and *Africa Is a Country*. She wrote the documentary *Across the Tracks: A Las Vegas Westside Story*. Her essay about leaving the United States for Jamaica after George Floyd's murder received a notable mention in *The Best American Essays 2023*.

Lorne Daniel is a Canadian poet and nonfiction writer living on unceded lands of the Lək'ʷəŋən people in Victoria, British Columbia. His most recent poetry collection, *What Is Broken Binds Us* (University of Calgary Press, 2025), includes poems on family estrangement, his American ancestors' involvement in enslavement, and recovery in a broken body. Daniel has been deeply engaged in Canadian literary communities since the 1970s, publishing five books, editing anthologies and literary journals, and writing freelance journalism. www.lornedaniel.ca

---

Lindsey Danis writes fiction and essays on travel, queer joy, and queer history. Her nonfiction book *(Out) On the Road: How Queer Travel Is Different and Why It Matters* is forthcoming. Danis's essays have appeared in *Condé Nast Traveler*, *AFAR*, Fodor's, and *Longreads*, been named a notable mention in *The Best American Travel Writing*, and appeared in several anthologies. When not writing, Danis is often found hiking or kayaking near her Hudson Valley home.

Michelle Dowd is the author of *Forager: Field Notes for Surviving a Family Cult*, a memoir about growing up in an apocalyptic cult and reclaiming her life through wildness, beauty, and the body. Her work appears in *The New York Times*, the *Los Angeles Times*, *The Alpinist*, and other national publications.

She writes at the intersection of ecology, myth, and self-trust, helping others remember who they are through story, ritual, and land connection. Dowd is the founder of Forager Wildlife. Subscribe to her Substack at mdowd.substack.com for weekly field notes from the untamed path.

Nick Flynn's most recent book is *Low* (Graywolf, 2023). His bestselling memoir *Another Bullshit Night in Suck City* (Norton, 2004) was made into a film starring Robert De Niro (Focus Features, 2012) and has been translated into fifteen languages.

Stephanie Foo is the *New York Times* bestselling author of *What My Bones Know: A Memoir of Healing from Complex Trauma*. She has written for *Vox* and *The New York Times*. She worked as a radio producer for *This American Life* and *Snap Judgment*, and her stories aired on *Reply All*, *99% Invisible*, and *Invisibilia*. A noted speaker and instructor, she has taught at Columbia University and has spoken at venues from the Sundance Film Festival to the Missouri Department of Mental Health.

Gabriela Denise Frank is a literary artist, editor, educator, and winner of the Fern Academy Prize. Her writing, interviews, and visual art have appeared in *BOMB Magazine*, *Poet Lore*, *EcoTheo Review*, *Chicago Review*, *Epoch*, *DIAGRAM*, *Northwest Review*, *The Rumpus*, and elsewhere. The author of *How to Not Become the Breaking* (Gateway Literary Press, 2025), she serves as creative nonfiction editor of *Crab Creek Review*. www.gabrieladenisefrank.com

---

Susan Ito is the author of the memoir *I Would Meet You Anywhere*, published by the Ohio State University Press, a finalist for the National Book Critics Circle Award and the William Saroyan International Prize for Writing. She coedited the literary anthology *A Ghost at Heart's Edge: Stories & Poems of Adoption*. Her work has appeared in *Literary Mama*, *Catapult*, *Hyphen*, *The Bellevue Literary Review*, *AGNI*, *Guernica*, and elsewhere. She has been awarded residencies at MacDowell, the Mesa Refuge, Hedgebrook, and Blue Mountain Center. Her theatrical adaption of *Untold*, stories of reproductive stigma, was produced at Brava Theater.

Danielle Jernigan is a writer and Buddhist-inspired meditation guide and the founder of Ink & OM Studio, a contemplative space for women in mother-wound recovery. A former community doula and maternal mental health peer counselor, her work helps parent survivors of childhood abuse reimagine love as a capacity, not a performance. Her essays have appeared in *The New York Times* parenting newsletter, *YourTango*, and *The Nourishing Word Blog*. Her current project blends memoir and cultural critique to explore how modern self-love culture fails survivors. Learn more at www.daniellejernigan.com.

---

noam keim is a trauma worker, medicine maker, and flâneur freak. Their first essay collection, *The Land Is Holy*, was a 2024 Foreword Indies Bronze winner. keim's writing has been supported by Lambda Literary, Tin House, Sewanee, Roots.Wounds.Words, and Periplus, and they have been awarded residencies by Space A Kathmandu, Pocoapoco Oaxaca, and Nawat Fes among others. Their work can be found in the *Michigan Quarterly Review*, *ALOCASIA*, *The Massachusetts Review*, *The Kenyon Review*, and others. Connect on Instagram at @noamkeim or at noamkeim.com.

Erika Krouse is the author of four books of fiction and nonfiction, including her new short story collection, *Save Me, Stranger.* Her memoir, *Tell Me Everything: The Story of a Private Investigation*, was a *New York Times* Editors' Choice and winner of the Colorado Book Award and Housatonic Book Award. Krouse is a two-time winner of the Edgar Award, and her fiction has appeared in *The New Yorker, The Atlantic*, and elsewhere. Krouse mentors for the Book Project and the Portfolio Year at Lighthouse Writers Workshop, where she received the Beacon Award for Teaching Excellence.

Monique Laban is a writer from New York. Her work has appeared in *Electric Literature*, *The Offing*, *Clarkesworld*, and elsewhere. She has received support from Hedgebrook, the Center for Fiction, the Sewanee Writers' Conference, the Kenyon Review Writers Workshop, the Tin House Summer Workshop, Viable Paradise, and VONA.

Cassandra Lewis is a recipient of the PEN America/L'Engle Rahman Prize for Mentorship and was awarded an Individual Artist Fellowship from the Delaware Division of the Arts, a state agency in partnership with the National Endowment for the Arts. She has contributed to *The New Yorker, The New York Times, Electric Literature*, *The Rumpus*, *The Belladonna Comedy*, and *Broad Street Review.* She earned an MFA in writing from New College of California. Her debut narrative nonfiction manuscript, *The Biting Kind*, was short-listed for the SFWP Literary Awards. More information can be found on CassandraLewis.com.

Kate Lewis's work has been nominated for Best of the Net, appears in *The New York Times*, *The Washington Post*, *The Wall*

Street Journal, and more, and has been supported by time at the Sewanee Writers' Conference and the Virginia Center for the Creative Arts. She is online at @katehasthoughts, and at Substack, she writes The Village, conversations on craft and community.

Nicole Graev Lipson is the author of the *USA Today* bestselling memoir in essays *Mothers and Other Fictional Characters*. Her writing has appeared in *The Sun*, *Virginia Quarterly Review*, *The Gettysburg Review*, *River Teeth*, *Alaska Quarterly Review*, *Los Angeles Review of Books*, *The Washington Post*, and *The Boston Globe*, among other venues. Her work has been awarded a Pushcart Prize, selected for *The Best American Essays 2024*, and short-listed for a National Magazine Award. Originally from New York City, she lives outside of Boston with her family.

Tiffany Aldrich MacBain is a professor in the English department at the University of Puget Sound, where she teaches writing, editing, and nineteenth-century American literature. Her scholarly work on the archived travel diaries and life writing of Progressive Era artist Abby Williams Hill appears in *Legacy: A Journal of American Women Writers* and *Tulsa Studies in Women's Literature*. MacBain also writes personal essays about her experiences as a mother and a daughter and is coauthoring a series of mystery novels set in the Pacific Northwest, featuring a middle-aged academic who moonlights as a forensic linguist and amateur sleuth.

Jamal Mahjoub was born in London and has since lived in a number of cities, including Cairo, Århus, Paris, Barcelona, and currently Amsterdam. His work has won critical acclaim and has been widely translated. He writes literary fiction, crime fiction (as Parker Bilal), and creative nonfiction. His work has appeared in *Granta*, *The Guardian*, *The New York Times*, *Le Monde*, as well as various other publications. He is the recipient of several awards including the Guardian African Short Story Prize, the NH Vargas Llosa prize (Spain), and the Etonnants Voyageurs Prize (France). He was long-listed for the Theakstons Old Peculier Prize and the RSL Ondaatje Prize, and short-listed for the Prix Le Point du Polar Européen and the Caine Prize.

Onita Morgan-Edwards holds an MFA in creative writing from Ashland University. Her work has appeared in *Mom Egg Review*, *Facing Gun Violence: It's Always Close to Home for Someone*, *Glide Literary Magazine*, *A Gathering of Flowers: An Anthology in Essay*, and *Family Justice Journal*. Morgan-Edwards was the second-place winner in the Dayton Metro Library Poetry Contest (adult category) in 2025. She is an amateur photographer and adjunct professor of English at a community college in Ohio. Visit her at OnitaMorganEdwards.com.

Emi Nietfeld is the author of *Acceptance* (Penguin Press, 2022), a memoir of her journey through foster care and homelessness, interrogating the true meanings of resilience, ambition, and success. Today, Nietfeld writes about inequality and families for *The New York Times*, *The Atlantic*, *New York Magazine*, and other publications. Hailing from Minnesota, she lives in New York with her family.

Geneva Phillips is a 2025 Writing Freedom Fellow and the author of the memoir *Disappearing in Glimpses* (Mongrel Empire Press, 2020). She cofacilitates with Poetic Justice, a nationally recognized nonprofit that helps incarcerated women find their voices and discover hope and empowers change through writing in community.

Deesha Philyaw's debut short story collection, *The Secret Lives of Church Ladies*, won the 2021 PEN/Faulkner Award for Fiction, the 2020/2021 Story Prize, and the 2020 *Los Angeles Times* Book Prize: The Art Seidenbaum Award for First Fiction and was a finalist for the 2020 National Book Award for Fiction. Philyaw's debut novel, *The True Confessions of First Lady Freeman*, is forthcoming from Mariner Books, an imprint of HarperCollins, in 2026.

Anna Qu is a Chinese American writer. Her critically acclaimed debut memoir, *Made In China: A Memoir of Love and Labor*, was named a *New York Times* Editors' Choice pick. Her essays have appeared in *The Threepenny Review*, *Lumina*, *Kartika*, and *Kweli Journal*, among others. She was a 2023 Black Mountain Institute Shearing Fellow and has received support from Yaddo and Ragdale. She teaches at New England College and the Book Project at Lighthouse Writers Workshop and recently moved to Denver with her partner and their two cats.

Domenica Ruta is the *New York Times* bestselling author of the memoir *With or Without You* and the novels *Last Day*, a *New York Times* Notable Book of the year, and *All the Mothers*. She coedited the anthology *We Got This: Solo Mom Stories of Grit, Heart, and Humor*. She's published short fiction and essays in the *Iowa Review*, the *Boston Review*, the *Indiana Review*, *Epoch*, *Ninth Letter*, *The Cut*, *People*, and elsewhere, and has been anthologized a handful of times, most recently in *Wanting*.

Oslyn Serratos (pseudonym) is a Pacific Northwest city planner and a published journalist and historian. Serratos holds undergraduate degrees in journalism and history from the University of Southern California, and master's degrees in historic preservation and urban planning from Columbia University. Her work is inspired by her experiences breaking generational cycles as a first-generation, multiracial, multicultural woman. She has published research for the World Monuments Fund, the National Register of Historic Places, and SurveyLA. Her poetry appears in *We Need a Reckoning* (Blue Cactus Press, 2021) and the online journals *The Bijou Poetry Review* and *amphibi.us*.

Alyson Shelton is an award-winning screenwriter and essayist. Her writing is published at outlets including *The New York Times*, *Ms.*, and *The Rumpus*. She's a coeditor and contributor to *The Loss of a Lifetime: Grieving Siblings Share Stories of Love, Loss, and Hope*. Shelton is best known for her Instagram Live series inspired by George Ella Lyon's poem "Where I'm From," which celebrated its 200th episode in summer 2025.

Cheryl Strayed is the author of the #1 *New York Times* bestseller *Wild: From Lost to Found on the Pacific Crest Trail*, which was made into an Oscar-nominated film. Her bestselling collection of Dear Sugar columns, *Tiny Beautiful Things*, was adapted for an Emmy-nominated television show and as a play that has been staged in theaters around the world. Strayed is also the author of the critically acclaimed novel *Torch* and the bestselling collection *Brave Enough*. Her award-winning essays and stories have appeared in *The Best American Essays*, *The New York Times*, and elsewhere. She lives in Portland, Oregon.

Mattilda Bernstein Sycamore is the author, most recently, of *Touching the Art*, finalist for a Washington State Book Award and a Pacific Northwest Book Award. Her previous title, *The Freezer Door*, was a *New York Times* Editors' Choice and a finalist for the PEN/Jean Stein Book Award. Winner of a Lambda Literary Award and an American Library Association Stonewall Honor Book, she's the author of seven books, and editor of six anthologies, most recently *Between Certain Death and a Possible Future: Queer Writing on Growing Up with the AIDS Crisis*. Sycamore's new novel, *Terry Dactyl*, is just out from Coffee House Press.

Raksha Vasudevan is a writer and former aid worker. She has reported stories of race, environmental justice, and "progress" for *The New York Times*, *VICE*, *The Guardian*, *Outside*, *WIRED*, and *High Country News*, where she was also a contributing editor. Her essays and commentary on colonial legacy and family estrangement appear in *The New York Times Magazine*, *Harper's Bazaar*, *Guernica*, *Hazlitt*, *The Washington Post*, and *Literary Hub*, among others. Her debut nonfiction book, *Empires Between Us*, is forthcoming from Graywolf Press and Knopf Canada.

Jane Wong is the author of the memoir *Meet Me Tonight in Atlantic City* (Tin House, 2023). She also wrote two poetry collections: *How to Not Be Afraid of Everything* (Alice James, 2021) and *Overpour* (Action Books, 2016). She is the recipient of a Pushcart Prize and fellowships and residencies from the US Fulbright Program, Harvard's Woodberry Poetry Room, Artist Trust, Hedgebrook, Ucross, Loghaven, the Barbara Deming Memorial Fund, and others. She grew up in a Chinese American takeout restaurant on the Jersey shore and is an associate professor at Western Washington University.

Kristen Millares Young is a prize-winning journalist, essayist, and the author of the novel *Subduction*, named a staff pick by *The Paris Review.* Published by Red Hen Press, *Subduction* won Nautilus and IPPY awards and was a finalist for two International Latino Book Awards. On October 6, 2026, Red Hen Press will release her memoir-in-essays *Desire Lines.* Called "searching, generous, and unrelenting" by Melissa Febos, "alive with style and poetic lyricism" by Weike Wang, and "explosive and daring" by Luis Alberto Urrea, *Desire Lines* is a forensic investigation into the emotional topography of being a woman, a writer, and a mother. @kristenmillares

---

Resources

BOOKS

- *Shadow Daughter: A Memoir of Estrangement*, Harriet Brown (2018)
- *The Power of Parting: Finding Peace and Freedom Through Family Estrangement*, Eamon Dolan (2025)
- *Drama Free: A Guide to Managing Unhealthy Family Relationships*, Nedra Glover Tawwab (2023)
- *It's Them, Not You: How to Break Free from Toxic Parents and Reclaim Your Story*, Josh Connolly (2025)
- *Family Estrangement: A Matter of Perspective*, Kylie Agllias (2017)
- *Adult Survivors of Toxic Family Members: Tools to Maintain Boundaries, Deal with Criticism, and Heal from Shame After Ties Have Been Cut*, Sherrie Campbell, PhD (2022)

NEWSLETTERS

- *Estranged*, Maggie Frank-Hsu, maggiefrankhsu.substack.com
- *Bad Mothers*, Monica Cardenas, monicacardenas.substack.com
- *Family Estrangement*, Tam Stevens, familyestrangement.substack.com

SOCIAL MEDIA

- **@sitwithwhit**, Whitney Goodman, LMFT
- **@therapy.with.josh**, Josh Frank, LMSW
- **@motherwoundproject**, Stephi Wagner
- **@nate_postlethwait**, Nate Postlewaith
- **@patrickteahanofficial**, Patrick Teahan
- **@drbeccabland**, Dr Becca Bland
- **@healing.and.cptsd**, CPTSD Community for Complex Trauma Survivors
- **@therapyjeff**, Jeff Guenther, LPC

- **@drdoylesays**, Dr Glenn Patrick Doyle
- **@dr_sharon_martin**, Dr Sharon Martin, LCSW

SUPPORT GROUPS

- **Estranged & Thriving: Support for Adult Children** www.facebook.com/groups/estrangedandthriving
- **Sibling Estrangement: Sharing, Coping, Connecting** www.facebook.com/groups/688926101896419
- **Scapegoat Adult Children of Narcissistic Families** www.facebook.com/groups/779199269159916

ORGANIZATIONS

- **Together Estranged**, www.togetherestranged.org
- **Calling Home**, www.callinghome.co
- **Stand Alone**, www.standalone.org.uk
- **Family Support Resources**, www.familysupportresources.com

REFERENCED IN THE INTRODUCTION

- **Cornell Family Estrangement & Reconciliation Project** founded by Karl Pillemer, PhD, www.familyreconciliation.org
- **"How Estrangement Has Become an Epidemic in America"** by Joshua Coleman and Will Johnson in *Time*, time.com/7201531/family-estrangement-us-politics-epidemic-essay
- **"Oprah Explores the Rising Trend of Going No Contact with Your Family"** on *The Oprah Podcast*, www.youtube.com/watch?v=cK7EJgILMIk

Permissions

"The Cost of a Mother" by Hannah Bae. A previous version of this essay appeared in *Pigeon Pages*, 2019. Used with permission of the author.

"Episodic Tremor and Slip" by Lorne Daniel. Excerpted with permission from *What Is Broken Binds Us*, published by University of Calgary Press, 2025.

"Father Outside" by Nick Flynn. Excerpted from *Some Ether: Poems*. Copyright © 2000 by Nick Flynn. Reprinted with the permission of The Permissions Company, LLC, on behalf of Graywolf Press, Minneapolis, Minnesota, graywolfpress.org.

"The Stripping of Threads" by Jamal Mahjoub. Originally published in *Granta* #161, 2022. Used with permission of the author.

"Whiting" by Deesha Philyaw. Originally published in *Slush Pile Magazine* #23, 2018. Used with permission of the author.

"The Empty Bowl" by Cheryl Strayed. Excerpted from *Tiny Beautiful Things: Reese's Book Club: Advice on Love and Life from Dear Sugar* by Cheryl Strayed. Copyright © 2012 by Cheryl Strayed. Used by permission of Vintage Books, an imprint of the Knopf Doubleday Publishing Group, a division of Penguin Random House LLC. All rights reserved.

"The Many Meanings of Family Estrangement" by Raksha Vasudevan. Originally published in *Harper's Bazaar*, January 19, 2022. Used by permission of Harper's Bazaar, Hearst Magazine Media, Inc.

© Devon Michelle

Jenny Bartoy is a French American writer, critic, and editor. Her work appears in *The Seattle Times*, *The Boston Globe*, *Chicago Review of Books*, *CrimeReads*, *The Rumpus*, *Room*, and other publications, as well as in several anthologies. She holds a master's degree in sociocultural anthropology from Columbia University. She lives in the Pacific Northwest with her family.